UPON THIS ROCK

A Life Story Of Simon Peter

John Hibbert

authorHOUSE®

AuthorHouse™
1663 Liberty Drive
Bloomington, IN 47403
www.authorhouse.com
Phone: 1-800-839-8640

First published by AuthorHouse 11/16/2010

ISBN: 978-1-4520-4638-9 (sc)

Printed in the United States of America

Certain stock imagery © Thinkstock.

This book is printed on acid-free paper.

INTRODUCTION

MANY WONDERFUL LITERARY WORKS HAVE been produced concerning the life of the Apostle Paul. They were made possible by the abundance of information available through the writings of the New Testament and other historical documents. Men like Luke have left us a diary of events, listing Paul's travels and activities, for us all to read and study. Peter, however, had no scribe accompanying him throughout his years of service and we have no documents relating to his life. Early historical works, which would have furnished us with some details, have disappeared. In 303 AD the Roman Emperor Diocletian commanded the destruction of all Christian writings and, tragically, much valuable history was lost. This marked the beginning of "The Great Persecution." The lack of detailed information has resulted in very little writing being attempted about the life of this foundation apostle of

John Hibbert

Jesus Christ and a loss of the potential inspiration which his story provides for today's church.

I have attempted to write a semi-fictionalised account of Simon Peter's life story, using the information given to us in the New Testament, reading between the lines, making some calculated assumptions and applying some imagination. As for the obscure years, I have used small signposts about Peter, which are given by Paul in his letters, to piece together some of his movements. We learn from Paul that Peter's wife travelled with him and that he had obviously visited Corinth. I have also used Peter's own writings. For example, I consider it reasonable to assume that the missionary journey's which he undoubtedly made, followed, at least to some degree, the list of the churches addressed in his first letter and must have taken him several years to complete and involved him travelling several thousands of miles. I have also borrowed some church traditions to complete my story.

Although some protest that there is no evidence that Peter ever went to Rome, it is historically clear from second century writings that the universal church believed that Peter died in Rome, and that men of historic integrity, like Dionysius of Corinth, Clement of Alexandria, Tertullian, Jerome and Eusebius, all clearly believed that Peter spent some years preaching and teaching in Rome. (i)

For ease of reading I have presumed to give Peter's wife a name. I have called her Joanna, meaning "The Lord is Grace" because she not only drew on His grace through many years of difficulty and suffering, but also demonstrated it to those around her.

vi

Peter was an ordinary man, from a very ordinary background. He had no great education or earthly pedigree, but he developed into an extraordinary servant of Jesus Christ. It is my hope and prayer that this short account of his life might inspire others, who, like me, have no great qualifications as far as this world is concerned, to follow in the footsteps of this man, who truly followed in those of his Lord, that together we might win our generation for Christ.

PROLOGUE

"Each one of us is granted a short space in time;

A brief moment is our privilege, our destiny;

Wisdom cries for us to use it well,

For soon it will be gone;

Our name a mere memory on this temporal stage;

Its usefulness, not measured by the quantity of minutes lived,

But by the usage of those moments,

By the footprints that we leave, as signposts for posterity."

D AYLIGHT WAS FADING AS SIMON Peter walked thoughtfully up the long flight of steps which led from the narrow street, the site of today's Wailing Wall, opposite the Temple Mount, to the high iron gate of the fortress Antonia, a spectacular stone edifice which was built on a rocky precipice by Herod the Great in 36 BC. He was escorted by no less than sixteen Roman guards who led him unceremoniously through the gates of the impressive building, which now served as a barracks for the occupying Roman forces. Six hundred Roman soldiers were billeted in the fortress which overlooked the Jewish Temple, another magnificent achievement of the notorious King of the Jews, who died in 4 BC. The prisoner, who was being led to his incarceration on the orders of Herod Agrippa 1, grandson of

Herod the Great and descendant of the Jewish Hasmonean dynasty through his grandmother Marianne, looked somewhat pensive and disturbed, not because he was afraid, but because this particular journey, to this particular prison, conjured up memories he constantly struggled to forget. This was the place, to which troops of the Fulminata Legion garrison, had led his friend and master, Jesus of Nazareth, to answer before Pontius Pilate following His arrest in the Garden of Gethsemane and subsequent appearance before Caiaphas, the high priest. Though he knew that he was long since forgiven for his crime of denial and betrayal on that dreadful night, it did not take much for the old feelings of remorse and self recrimination to surface and torment his mind. These were the same steps which Jesus had climbed to the place of judgement and Peter's mind imagined the scene which he had been too cowardly to witness first hand.

It was the year 44 AD and Herod Agrippa had begun a telling persecution of the church in Jerusalem. The new emperor of Rome, Caligula, had made him governor over the province of Palestine as a puppet king. As anything was preferable to direct Roman rule, Agrippa was popular with the people and was determined to do everything to please them. The setting up of his palace in Jerusalem was widely applauded and the new upsurge of opposition against the Christian church gave him further opportunity to gain favour with the people. The church, which now numbered thousands in the city, was never popular with religious Jews, but the recent inclusion of Gentiles into the Christian fold was, for them, most certainly a step too far and poured fuel onto the fires of hatred. Herod saw his opportunity and made his move. First he arrested James, the son of Zebedee, lifelong friend of Simon Peter, and one of the three most trusted and intimate disciples of Jesus. James was accused of subversion and sentenced to death. His execution by decapitation sent a wave of horror through the Christian community and Peter suffered the anguish of personal bereavement. He struggled to understand why God allowed the death of one who was so important to His Kingdom, but sought, nevertheless, to comfort James' mother, Salome and her other son John, in their tragic loss. There were many tears and much apprehension for the future. It seemed good to all of the apostolic team, that Mary the mother of Jesus, should be taken to a place of safety and John, the brother of James, was the obvious one to accompany her, as he was commissioned by Jesus from His cross to take care of His mother. It seemed that hatred and persecution were producing an era of "good-byes" and some of them were final. Peter would have given a great deal to step back in time and take one more excursion onto his beloved Lake Galilee with his two friends, like the old days, to feel the exhilarating spray in his face and laugh with James and John in the face of the storm. He also knew, however, that this was no time for self pity, or for looking back. If the church in Jerusalem was to survive this present storm, it needed strong leadership and a display of faith from the apostles. James would have been the first to encourage boldness and trust in the face of adversity.

Unknown to the apostles, Agrippa was being congratulated from all quarters for his brave and forthright execution of one of the most prominent of the church leaders and was being encouraged to go further. Relishing the possibility of increased popularity and acclaim, he turned his attention to the one known as Simon Peter, probably the most well known and outspoken Christian leader in Jerusalem. What a prize it would be for the enemies of Jesus of Nazareth, if James's friend Peter, was to follow him to the block. It would be a cruel and, hopefully, a terminal blow against these Christian fanatics. So with rising confidence Herod issued the arrest warrant and Peter found himself on an imposed journey to the prison cell.

The dark bowels of Fortress Antonia, so named after Agrippa's friend Mark Anthony, were a far cry from the beautiful sun-bathed exterior. Peter was led down three flights of steps, past two checkpoints, along a dimly lit corridor, and was finally manhandled into a gloomy cell, which was actually cut into the original rock face of the hill. A single torch, flickering nervously from a metal wall-bracket, was the only light and the smell of damp, stale air and untreated sewage, made it difficult to breathe freely. It was so cold. Despite the fact that a substantial metal gate secured the room, the soldiers proceeded to anchor Peter into a corner with heavy chains. To his surprise two of the guards then chained themselves to their prisoner, one on each side, and set themselves to wait out the rest of their shift. Two more sat outside the locked gate of the cell. Perhaps Herod had heard stories about previous occasions when the Jewish leaders had tried to imprison this man, but he was certainly taking every precaution to maximise security.

"This is where they brought him you know."

The words came from the older of the two guards. He spoke casually, as though to make idle conversation. Peter had wondered if this was the cell where his friend James had spent his final hours. The guard's words gave him a strange sense of fellowship with his departed comrade and even a modicum of comfort. The man's next words destroyed it.

"They brought him in here briefly before the scourging and then afterwards before they crucified him." The Roman shuddered. "He was a bloody mess. If you look closely, with the torch, you can still see blood-stains in the stone wall over there."

Peter's heart rate quickened and a lump rose in his throat, as the realisation dawned upon him that the soldier was not referring to James, but was talking about Jesus. He was sitting in the very place where the Lord had sat, before He was taken to Golgotha to die. Suddenly Peter was living again those dreadful hours in the judgement hall of Caiaphas and replaying in his mind the words of denial which had spilled from his lips as he betrayed his Lord. How ironic that he should now go to his death from the same prison cell as the One he had failed. He remembered the words of Jesus on the beach of Lake Galilee, after He had provided them with breakfast, on the morning of his restoration.

"When you are old," He said, "another shall gird thee and carry thee wither thou wouldest not."

Peter knew at the time that Jesus was prophesying for him, a martyr's death. The fulfilment of that prophesy was now taking place. He had been led to this place against his will. He was not exactly old, but several years had gone by and he was now considerably older than Jesus was when He was crucified. Within a few days he was going to die and, tragically, he did not feel ready.

Peter made no reply to his unlikely companion. His mind was a whirlpool of swirling thoughts, feelings and emotions. He wished he had done more for His Lord. Jesus said, "Go into all the world and preach the Gospel," and he had not done it. There was so much to do, so many people to reach and he felt that he had squandered his opportunity. He wondered if God would somehow rescue him from his fate and give him another chance, but he did not believe it in his heart. After all, God had not rescued James, now dead, who Peter considered far more worthy than himself. He was now destined to stand before his Lord in the eternal world, as much a failure as an evangelist, as he had been as a friend on the night of his betrayal of the Christ.

He thought of his lovely wife, Joanna, and the sorrow and bereavement she would feel at his loss. Perhaps he should have spent more time with her. It seemed as though he had spent the whole of his early life working at expanding his fishing business and the rest working for the church. He was plagued with guilt. He felt the biggest failure in the world. The depressive atmosphere of his cold confinement overwhelmed him. He suddenly felt too weary to care and fell into a fitful sleep.

He dreamed of beautiful Galilee and succulent green pastures rolling back from the lakes placid waters. He absorbed the smells of fresh fish cooking on open fires on the shingle shores and the laughter of children playing at the water's edge. He dreamed of James when he was a little boy and watched him climbing on his father's moored fishing boat and screaming with delight as he leaped from the bows into the shallow water. He dreamed of His wonderful friend Jesus preaching to the people as they sat in their thousands on the grassy slopes. He dreamed of black, lowering, storm clouds on a hill called Golgotha and of huge ugly vultures hovering, waiting for life to depart. He saw a hooded figure and a raised sword. He saw the head of his friend James, eyes still open, rolling in the dust. He sobbed in his sleep and his weeping woke him.

They fed him a scant breakfast and four more soldiers replaced the first quaternion. Peter did not feel good. He found it difficult to discard the pathos of his night dreams and find a footing in the real world. It did not feel like the real world in this hell-hole of a place. He wanted to know when he was going to die; at least that would enable him to prepare for the moment. He asked the soldier to his left. The reply was yet another shock to his system.

"I don't know, it's Passover in a few days, I would think it will be soon after the feast."

Peter felt a physical wave of horror gallop through his body, as he realised that he was going to die at the Jewish Feast of Passover, the anniversary of the crucifixion of Jesus. Not only was he to be led to his death from the same cell, but at the same symbolic occasion as his Lord. The irony of it all slammed into his emotions with crippling effect. He looked with wide-eyed astonishment into the eyes of his guard. The horror of the parallels between him and the experience of his Lord jolted him into positive action. If he was going to die he would at least give the Gospel to his captors. He asked for the attention of the two who were chained to him, as well as the two who manned the gate, and for the next two hours he shared with them his amazing story. From the fishing boats of home, to his first meeting with Jesus, the miracles and the teaching and the story and meaning of Christ crucified. He told them of the resurrection of Jesus and the coming of the Holy Spirit on the day of Pentecost and the growth of the church. He felt better afterwards. Preaching the Gospel always seemed to feed his own spirit.

John Hibbert

Four days later Peter was informed that the following morning he would be executed by decapitation with the sword. Mid-afternoon, he was informed that he had a visitor and a tearful Joanna was shown into the poorly lit cell. The soldiers at first refused to unshackle their prisoner, but after some pleading from Peter, the men extricated themselves from his chains and joined their companions on the other side of the gate.

Husband and wife were instantly locked in fond embrace, silent, but for the gentle weeping which overflowed from both their hearts. They held each other, without a word passing between them, for such a length of time that Peter's captors began to grow nervous with suspicion. Their eyes pierced the gloom in search of evidence of intrigue, but they saw only love. Peter finally broke the silence.

"Don't mourn for me, my love. I am an unworthy servant of my Lord. I count it a privilege to die in His cause. I am only sorry to leave you in your grief, but I know that the God we know and love, will care for you always. Tell the people of His church that I love them and will pray for their expansion and protection with my dying breath."

"But Peter, they are all praying for you, that God will rescue you from death. All over the city, in houses across Jerusalem, prayer is being made for your deliverance. You must not give up."

Peter smiled sadly, "We all prayed for James, my love, a man more worthy than I, but he was not spared. There comes a time for this life to end. I have no complaints. I am at peace."

He took her once more into his arms and his lips pressed down upon her own. She opened them in one last expression of intimacy and mutual love flowed with their shared breath.

"I love you more than words could ever say Joanna. Farewell my love, until we meet beyond the veil."

She whispered her last "I love you" and turned to the gate of his cell. The guard opened it and she walked through and away down the corridor without looking back. Tears of bitter heart-ache flowed down her grief-stricken face.

Peter ate his supper of bread and cheese with an accompanying cup of wine, smuggled in by his guards. He lay down to sleep with a faint smile upon his lips. He was ready. His next meal would be in the presence of his Lord.

CHAPTER ONE

_____

"Despising not base origins;
Nor contemptuous of a mind unlearned,
Perceiving, deep within, a heart to train;
You took my hand and changed my name"

SIMON BAR JONAS WAS BORN five years before Christ in a small fishing village named Bethsaida on the northern shore of Lake Galilee. His father was a fisherman and consequentially Simon and his brother Andrew were brought up to love the lake and its wildlife and the commerce surrounding it. His earliest memories were of water and boats and fish and he was swimming like one before he was five. As a tiny boy he sat for hours at the water's edge, scooping up the crystal clear water in his hands, watching it run through his fingers, laughingly hurling it skyward to watch it fragment into a thousand bejewelled droplets in the light of the summer sun. He loved his father's fishing boat and was far too young when he spent his first day out on the lake with the men. By twelve years old he was occasionally spending whole nights on the boat, sometimes helping with the work and sometimes falling asleep on a pile of sackcloth in the stern. Whatever, there was no doubt where he loved to be and, although he went to school when he was six and learned to read and write like all his contemporaries, his

1

heart was out on the lake and his only ambition was to follow in the footsteps of his father.

Jonas taught his sons carefully to be skilled exponents of his trade, how to keep the ship in good repair, how to tend and mend the nets, how to read the weather and how to discern when the lake was feeling peaceful and when it was likely to be angry. Simon learned to sense its mood. He formed a relationship with this unpredictable inland sea, which was sometimes friendly and sometimes combatant. It was the source of life and yet, when aroused, capable of serving up death. As a young teenager he often sat at the edge of the lake and drank in the beauty of the dawn and watched as the first rays of the sun gently kissed the still surface of the water. He was at home with this amazing Sea of Galilee and its lush surroundings. He experienced a feeling of awe as he surveyed the rugged mountains to the east and marvelled at the droplets of dew which glistened, fresh from the womb of the morning, on the many moss-mantled rocks at the edge of the water. He loved the slopping noise as the water rippled against the stones.

He breathed the smell of the fish. He enjoyed the creaking timber of the boat beneath his feet and he came to love the exhilaration of fighting the sudden violent storms which the lake was prone to throw up. He loved the thrill of the catch and the sting of the spray-filled wind in his face. When he returned home, whether in the evening, or early in the morning, he was a young man at peace with himself and the world, weary, but fulfilled. He grew into a man of transparent sincerity, outspoken, self-willed, brave, bold, hard working and stubbornly independent. He was utterly content. It would not be easy for any power on earth to prise this man from his chosen way of life.

Following the death of their parents, Simon and Andrew moved west along the coast to the city of Capernaum. On the north-western curve of the lake, Capernaum nestled at the edge of a lush little plain known in those days as the "land of Gennesaret" and had become a city of no mean importance, as a centre for trade, manufacturing and fishing industries. On the plain of Gennesaret, Capernaum shared an area of only four miles in length with two other communities, Chorazin and Bethsaida. Of these two, nothing now remains, whereas ruins of ancient Capernaum are still visible to the modern tourist, in the place now called Kefar Nahum. Strategically placed between the lake and the Via Maris, the main highway connecting Babylon to the east and with Egypt to the south, with its constant stream of trade bearing camels, Roman legions, pilgrims on their way to Jerusalem, and a complete diversity of people from every walk of life, Capernaum was no ordinary city. The attraction for Simon, however, did not lie in its human activity, but in its thriving fishing industry and its unparallel natural beauty. The land of Gennesaret was an area of astonishing natural attributes. The very name, meaning "garden of abundance" evokes a pleasing picture of nature's craftsmanship. And such it was, a veritable paradise of succulent greenery, colourful shrubs, diversities of trees and a profusion of flowers, all set like a pillow at the edge of a lake of awe-inspiring beauty. Birds, in abundance and variety, added nature's finishing touch. Multi-coloured kingfishers dived all day from overhanging branches for their unsuspecting prey, whilst ungainly looking pelicans skimmed the surface of the water with surprising ease. It was a place of tranquillity and beauty without equal anywhere in Israel. What better place was there on earth for a young man to ply his trade and fall in love? Fall in love he did, with a strikingly pretty local girl, named Joanna.

After their marriage, Simon and Joanna made their home in a spacious house not far from the water's edge and only a stone's throw away from the synagogue. Joanna's widowed mother and Simon's brother Andrew, lived with them.

Life was wonderful and Simon was content with his lot. He and Andrew formed a close friendship with two other young fishermen, James and John, the sons of a very prosperous fishing magnate named Zebedee and his wife Salome. A good natured competitive spirit was the cause of much banter and arguing about the size of the latest hauls of fish, and raucous laughter and occasional raised voices often filled the morning air. Sometimes Salome brought food to her husband and sons as they mended their nets and the brothers introduced her to their friends. On one occasion she brought her younger sister, Mary, to meet them. She was visiting from Nazareth and Simon and Andrew got to meet her young son, who was training to be a carpenter.

The years passed and business was good. Only one thing prevented the deepening of their contentment; the lack of offspring. Joanna so desperately wanted a baby and Peter longed to give her one, but their impassioned love-making bore no fruit. Although Simon was not a particularly religious person, he had read the Torah in his years at school and believed in the existence of God. He didn't believe enough to pray for a child, but he believed enough to use the existence of God as a means of offering possible comfort to his wife.

"Perhaps we are not intended to have a family, Joanna. Perhaps the God of Abraham has some other purpose for our lives, which does not include children. Or maybe you will have a baby when you are ninety years old, as did our mother Sarah."

He laughed at his own joke and drew a faint smile from his grieving wife. She believed a little more than he did in the God of their fathers.

"Perhaps He does have another purpose Simon. If so, then I suppose we should trust Him."

Simon smiled at his success, but as he did so, he had the strangest feeling, that what he had suggested and the reply she had given, were of more significance than he cared to believe. He silently scolded himself for indulging in religious sentiment. He was a fisherman and that's all he ever intended to be, and what possible purpose, other than catching fish, could there be in that?

He was a mature man of thirty eight years old when Andrew asked him one day if he would like to accompany him and his friend, John the son of Zebedee, on an excursion to the Jordan River, to meet the one known as John the Baptist. Simon was aware of his brother's fascination with this man, who was evidently preaching repentance from sin and announcing the imminent emergence of the Messiah. Reports told of a wild, prophet-like character, like a modern day Elijah, garbed with a camel-hair wrap, who lived on a diet of locusts and wild honey. He was said to be of a quite frightening appearance, but preached a compelling message, which he delivered with passion and conviction. Andrew came to know of him through the sons of Zebedee, because John the Baptist was the son of their mother's cousin, who was evidently married to a priest in Jerusalem. Andrew and John had already visited the preacher several times and now counted themselves amongst his close disciples. Someone else told Peter that every day people were now making pilgrimage, through the hostile Judean wilderness, to see and hear this strange phenomenon and those who embraced his message were being baptised in the river, as a symbol of their conversion. He did not really want to go, but he did want to please his brother.

"I'll go if James goes," he said reluctantly. Andrew smiled. He already had John working on that one.

The lake was calm and the night clear as the four men set out on their journey across the length of the Galilee. Although the crossing was smooth, the dawn was already breaking as they moored their boat at Deganya and set out on foot to make the almost fifty mile journey through the Jordan Valley. Their goal was the tiny village of Bethabara and night was falling on their second day of walking, as they wearily reached their destination. They found an adequate lodging house, which gave them a roof over their heads and mats on which to rest and within minutes the four of them were fast asleep. Simon woke momentarily at daybreak to witness his brother and John, creeping quietly out into the crisp morning air. He smiled to himself as he turned over and closed his eyes. Andrew had always been the excitable type. He couldn't wait to get to the river to see his prophet friend.

Andrew and John were at the baptismal site even before the Baptist arrived, but they were not the first. Already small groups of pilgrims were standing, conversing in low tones, waiting for the arrival of the preacher. When John arrived he came over and welcomed the brothers with exciting news concerning recent events at the river. Apparently, six weeks previously, another of John's cousins, Jesus of Nazareth, son of Salome's sister, Mary, visited John at the river and requested to be baptised by him. The ensuing ceremony resulted in the most amazing happenings. John told them how, as Jesus came up out of the water, a supernatural manifestation, in the form of a dove, alighted upon Jesus and, to the astonishment of the onlookers, a voice, like the voice of thunder from a stormy sky, spoke clearly the words, "Thou art my beloved Son, in whom I am well pleased."

Andrew remembered the morning when he first met the young Jesus, when his mother brought him to the lake.

"You mean Jesus, the one who was training to be a carpenter? You mean He is the Son of God? You mean He is the long awaited Messiah? Where is He now?"

"I don't know. He climbed up the bank, rung out his clothes, and left. He did not return until yesterday."

"But where is He now, John? I must see Him."

"I have no idea. He said he had been in the wilderness for forty days. Maybe He has returned to the desert places. He did not say and I did not ask. I do feel that something important has taken place though. It has left me with the feeling that the reason for my existence is now complete, that somehow my preaching has reached its fulfilment."

Andrew and John looked at each other with a mixture of excitement, that the Messiah could be close by and regret that they had not come a day sooner. They instinctively turned from the bank of the river and scanned the surrounding terrain in the hope that He might be standing there, but there was no-one. Over the next few hours they busied themselves in the work of the Baptist, helping people down into the river, and then back up the bank to dry clothes and warm conversation. The people came in a steady stream from, who knows where? Sometimes John was silent, speaking only in subdued undertones to his individual converts, before lowering them into the waters of the Jordan. At other times he lifted his voice and it echoed across the surface of the river, humbly telling the people of One who was greater than himself, whose shoes he was not worthy to fasten. The atmosphere was at once solemn, like the quietness of the temple's holy place, and then tingling with the power of declared truth.

The sun climbed to its zenith and Andrew and John decided that it was time to return to the lodging house and find Simon and James. They hoped to persuade them to come and meet John. The Baptist was taking a well earned break from the river and stood chatting to his Galilean visitors, promising prayers for their respective brothers. Suddenly he grasped Andrew's arm in a grip of steel and gestured with his head towards an approaching stranger. Nobody spoke, but two hearts pounded and two minds whirled with excitement and anticipation. A lone stranger was slowly approaching. He appeared no different from anybody else, but He was clothed with an aura of regal dignity. Andrew stood, motionless, as destiny embraced him. Could this really be the Christ? Was it possible that the One promised from centuries past, the Messiah, was actually walking towards them?

"Behold, the Lamb of God."

It was the voice of the prophet. That was all John said, but his words hung in the air, poignant, pregnant with meaning. They were strange, prophetic words, which the fishermen did not understand, but they were words which announced the arrival of the One who had been born to die, as the sacrificial lamb for the sins of the world. Their eyes were fastened on the approaching Jesus and they hesitatingly stepped forward to meet Him, but as they did so, to their surprise and consternation, he turned and climbed the path away from the river. He was walking away from them! He obviously had no intention of staying at the baptismal site, or of engaging in a conversation with John. Why then had He come? Why take the trouble to walk to the river, for so brief a moment? Could it possibly have anything to do with them? Was it some kind of Divine providence which brought Him to this place at this particular hour?

While the friends reasoned, the "Lamb of God", whatever that meant, was walking away. They felt awkward, confused and embarrassed, but they simultaneously made the decision to run after Him.

They walked like a pair of small boys behind Jesus, not knowing how to approach Him, or what to say. At first He did not turn, or acknowledge in any way that He knew that they were there, but eventually He stopped and turned to them, smiling.

"What seek ye?" He asked.

John took the initiative and replied, "Master, where dwellest Thou?"

Jesus smiled again and said, "Come and see."

They did, of course, enthusiastically agree, but time overtook them in their journey and it was past four in the afternoon before they finally arrived at the humble dwelling, which was the temporary home of the Messiah. All thought of Simon and James was now gone and they remained there with Jesus for the rest of the evening and for the whole of that night. Two fishermen and a carpenter talked of the great plan of Almighty God throughout the most amazing night that Andrew and John had ever known. They asked Him innumerable questions and marvelled at the insight which His answers revealed, concerning His future and theirs. Their hearts burned within them as they listened to Him talk of His Father and of things concerning the Kingdom. He expounded to them the mysteries of the scriptures, concerning the law and the prophets and God's purposes for the world. They finally left their meeting with Jesus as another dawn spread its light across the river valley. As they walked out into a new day, they both knew that they would never be the same again. How could they be?

Simon's traditional Jewish schooling included in depth teaching of Old Testament law, as well as the history of God's dealings with Israel, but he nevertheless developed a cynical scorn towards all things religious. He hated religious pomp and ceremony and was not at all disposed to listen to the endless philosophising of religious hypocrites. He viewed the religious leaders of the day, as men who laid upon their fellow men burdens too grievous to be borne, burdens which they were unwilling to carry themselves. Simon was a plain man, a man of the earth, or rather, of the sea. He believed in God, but preferred to feel Him in the spray thrown up by the bow of his boat and to see Him in the rugged beauty of the mountains. He was not impressed with his brother's fascination with this character

John the Baptist and his prolonged absence, for a day and a night, found him incubating a mixture of attitudes, ranging from extreme annoyance and anger, to brotherly concern for Andrew's welfare. James was far from happy either, and the appearance of their brothers, a full thirty hours after they had left, hurrying towards them, radiant and energised by their night with Jesus, served only to inflame the anger of the waiting pair.

It obviously took several minutes of explanation and apologising, before peace was restored between the friends and brothers, but even then, Simon was in no mood for visiting either the baptiser, or the carpenter. He just wanted to head north to the boat and home. It took some impassioned pleading from Andrew, before Simon eventually relented and a deal was struck. They would go and find Jesus of Nazareth, remain with Him for just a short while, and then they would head up the valley and take their boat back to Capernaum.

So it was that Simon bar Jonas, one destined to be one of the most valuable servants of God in the history of the early church, came face to face with Jesus for the first time. What a memorable meeting it was. The Messiah stood on the bank of the Jordan, just above the baptismal site, a lone figure, silhouetted against the blue sky. Physically, He was not extraordinary. Facially, He was just another Jewish male of around thirty years of age, sporting a traditional beard and the typical features of a son of Abraham. It was His eyes that were the striking feature of this amazing man. They were soft and kind and pure, but they were searching, penetrating eyes, which looked into the very soul of a man. Simon approached Him with the others and their eyes met. Instantly the fisherman melted inside. He suddenly felt inexplicably emotional. A lump rose in his throat and his heart pounded in his chest. Andrew spoke.

"Master, this is my brother Simon, and John's brother, James."

Jesus looked at Simon for what seemed like an eternity, then He spoke, softly, but with an insight and authority which was prophetic, compelling, almost frightening. There were no niceties, no introductory pleasantries.

He just said, "Thou art Simon son of Jonas. Thou shalt be called Cephas."

That was all that He said, but He continued to hold Simon's eyes, as though searching for his reaction. The fisherman said nothing! He was lost for words! What does one say when a complete stranger announces that one's name is to be changed? According to this One, who his brother believed to be the Messiah, he was going to be called Cephas (The Aramaic word for "Peter") instead of Simon, or maybe in addition to Simon. It was the strangest possible introduction to a stranger and Simon would normally have responded to such a weird and presumptuous declaration, with cutting humour, but the man's words were powerful, giving no opportunity for objection or debate. Simon shifted uncomfortably from one foot to the other. "Peter!" It means, "A rock." The name implied a change of character, responsibility, perhaps even vocation. The statement of Jesus conveyed a sense of destiny which troubled the older man. For a moment he felt as though this carpenter from Nazareth was interfering with his future and leaving him, in some mysterious way, without a choice. Towards the end of His ministry Jesus was to address Simon again about his name. He would ask His disciples, "Who do men say that I am?" and Simon Peter replied, "Thou art the Christ, the Son of the living God." Then Jesus made the statement which explained the reason for the change of the fisherman's name.

"Blessed art thou Simon bar Jonas, for flesh and blood hath not revealed it unto thee, but My Father which is in heaven. And I say also unto thee, that thou art Peter, and upon this rock I will build my church; and the gates of hell shall not prevail against it. And I will give unto thee the keys of the kingdom of heaven." (ii)

That day at Bethabara, Simon had no knowledge of the future, or that he would ever see this man again. He turned away and the quartet of fishermen experienced a mixture of emotions as they headed north, up the river valley, to return to the lake. Their conversation was concerning the Christ. Andrew and John talked together constantly about their unforgettable night with Jesus and the revelation which they had received, about the fulfilling of the law and the prophets. They speculated about the future of Israel and whether the Messiah would now rid them of the Roman occupation. James was more subdued, feeling a little left out of everything, and Simon was thoughtful and not a little troubled by the words of Jesus, which he seemed unable to shake out of his mind. "You will be called a rock."

They arrived at their moored boat and, under a clear moonlit sky, set sail to a favourable wind and came to Capernaum with good speed.

CHAPTER TWO

―――――――――

"Oh hollow lake of discontent;
Your hold on me has lost its power;
My fishing field is now the world,
My zeal to drag the devils sea;
My net, the Word, to fish for men"

S IMON IMMERSED HIMSELF IN HIS trade. He was
born to fish and Lake Galilee was one of the richest
fishing grounds in the world. Its coastline was heavily
populated, with villages and towns, large and small, nine of
them having populations of more than 15,000 people. As
everyone in Israel ate fish, Simon and Andrew prospered
through their expertise. They very often fished alone, but
when they were employing the long dragnets, it was easier
to haul the nets between two boats, so their friendship with
the sons of Zebedee had developed into an exciting business
partnership, as they plied their trade together. Night after
night the zealous fishermen launched their boats onto the
belly of the lake and rowed out into the cool darkness for
their harvest. When storms were brewing and more prudent
men of the sea stayed at home, Simon and his colleagues
took up the challenge of the elements and found an even
deeper satisfaction in bringing home their catch.

Simon was a determined, self-willed character, who, though constantly troubled with the memory of his meeting with Jesus of Nazareth, had no intentions of allowing an event, now in the past, to dominate his life and thinking. He had a wife to care for and a business to run. As days passed, he succeeded in shaking thoughts of the Messiah, and the impression He had left on him, from his mind.

The day following His meeting with the fishermen from Galilee, Jesus heard the shocking news that John the Baptist had been unexpectedly arrested and taken into prison. His reaction was unpredictable because, after hearing the news, Jesus made the strange decision to leave the area altogether and head north towards Galilee. He felt no great concern for His cousin, believing that this was only a temporary arrest, from which he would soon be released, an opinion about which circumstances were to prove Him right. He decided to head for His native Nazareth, but not before He had called Philip, another son of Bethsaida, and Nathaniel, to follow Him.

Nazareth was a despised city, not only by the people of the more prosperous south, but even amongst the Galileans. Despite its beautiful natural setting, it was, for some unknown reason, regarded with contempt by the whole of Israel. To Jesus, however, it was home. Here were the streets which He had frequented as a boy. Here was the place of His education, the homes of His friends, and the carpentry where He had spent so many happy years with Joseph. There was scarcely a home in the entire community, which did not have a chair or table which had been manufactured or repaired at Joseph's Carpentry. Here was the local synagogue, where His mother had taken Him as a child, which she had encouraged Him to appreciate and attend for His whole life and it was to the synagogue that He made His way, on the first Sabbath day, after His return from the Jordan. From the moment of His baptism, when he heard the voice of His Father by the river, He was conscious of His identity as never before. A feeling of urgency now gripped His heart, established even more deeply in His will, by the six weeks opposition He had endured in the wilderness. He was never more conscious of His calling and He was convinced that it was time for something new and wonderful to begin. He now knew, absolutely and without doubt, that He had arrived at the reason for His birth.

Many times throughout His years in Nazareth, He had mounted the 'Bema' (iii) in the synagogue, where the sacred scroll was laid upon the 'Luach', or lectern, and read from the Holy Scriptures. So it was not unusual for Him to take up His position and prepare to read. Whether it was His two months absence, or the aura of dignified authority which now cloaked the emerging Messiah, or an increase in the Divine Presence in the sanctum itself, there was an atmosphere of expectation in the crowded room that day, which was different from anything the people had experienced before. A hush fell upon the assembled Nazarenes, as Jesus chose a place in the writings of Isaiah the Prophet and began to read.

"The Spirit of the Lord is upon me, because He has anointed me to preach the Gospel to the poor; He hath sent me to heal the broken hearted, to preach deliverance to the captives, and recovering of sight to the blind, to set at liberty them that are bruised, to preach the acceptable year of the Lord."

17

He suddenly closed the book and walked slowly back to His seat. The silence of holiness permeated the synagogue. Every eye was fastened on Jesus. They knew this man, but they did not know anymore, who He was. They were suddenly in awe of their local carpenter. He had read the words of the prophet as though they were His own, written for Him six hundred years before He was born. Nobody moved. The Rabbi remained seated and every person in the building watched the Anointed One, as He sat with His head slightly bowed in the presence of His Father. Almost imperceptibly, His head began to lift and His eyes slowly scanned the astonished congregation. Then He spoke in a voice little more than a whisper, but his words echoed around the chamber.

"This day is this scripture fulfilled in your ears!"

That day Jesus left Nazareth forever! It was no longer His home. The carpentry now belonged to a past life. A new era had dawned and He began His final journey to the cross. His life of preparation for service was over. Now He was ready for active service. He left the town and travelled a few miles north to the city of Cana, where He attended the wedding of his Uncle Cleopas' son. There He performed His first miracle, by turning the water into wine. From there He headed for Capernaum on Lake Galilee, which was to become His new home, for the remainder of His ministry. He was accompanied by His mother, His brother James, Philip and Nathaniel. A spiritual dawn was breaking over the Galilee. The turning of the water into wine was the opening of the floodgates of God's power, as Jesus began to preach the Gospel of repentance and the arrival of the Kingdom of Heaven. The city was shaken by the power of the words of the man from Nazareth and the surrounding area was buzzing with news of miracles.

Simon was not pleased. He had no desire to be reminded of his meeting with Jesus, let alone come face to face with Him in his own community. He had an overwhelming sense of apprehension that, if he got too close to the Nazarene, it was going to bring serious upheaval into his life. He found himself investigating Jesus' movements, with the intent of avoiding Him. He was pleased when he heard that Jesus was preaching in some other community further round the coast, whilst at the same time, another part of him was curious. He felt drawn to Him, like the moth is drawn to the light, even though he knew he was going to get burnt. The negative prevailed, because, fundamentally, he was content with his life and did not want anything to change. He buried himself in his work. He felt safe when he was out at sea, outside the reach of those penetrating eyes, which had looked so deeply into his spirit at Bethabara. So he fished round the clock, working the nights, sleeping for a few hours in the afternoon, and then back to sea. Andrew's protests went unheeded and the money poured into the business.

The two brothers were standing knee deep in the lake one morning, casting their weighted nets into the water, when they heard a voice calling to them from the shingle beach behind them.

"Follow Me," He called, "and I will make you fishers of men."

The words were not so much a command, as a challenge, an offer of training to prepare for a higher form of employment. Simon froze. He knew, without turning round, who owned the voice and he knew that he had to obey. Andrew turned to witness the same scene that he had experienced two weeks before at the Jordan. Jesus was walking away. He was not going to ask twice. The challenge was issued and the choice was theirs. Without a moment's hesitation or contemplation, Andrew responded and began to splash his way out of the lake.

"Come on Simon! It's Jesus!"

Simon hesitated, momentarily. He really did not want to do this, but the same sense of excitement, which he had experienced at Bethabara, was flooding his spirit. Even as his mind hesitated, his legs were moving in the wake of his brother's. The nets were left jostling and tangling in the ebb and flow of the water.

The atmosphere was surreal as they walked westwards along the edge of the lake. Nobody spoke. Simon felt awkward and rather foolish. It was with some relief that he saw James and John, also casting their nets, just another hundred yards or so along the shore. Speaking to them would perhaps break the ice a little. As they approached, Jesus raised His hand slightly to Andrew and Peter, in a silent request for their silence and then called to the sons of Zebedee, that they also might follow Him. Without a word they also left their nets and, with an apologetic smile to their father, joined Simon and Andrew in their pursuit of Jesus. Over the next few days, these natural men seemed to leave the natural world and breathe the air of another Kingdom. They watched with awe, as Jesus revolutionised Capernaum with miracles. He delivered a man in the synagogue who was tormented by an unclean spirit, with a display of supernatural authority, which stunned and amazed the people and their religious leaders. He visited Simon's home and healed his mother-in-law of an infection, which had put her life in danger by plunging her into a raging fever. The following evening, as the sun was painting a slowly moving crimson path across Lake Galilee, the people came from everywhere, bringing their sick and diseased to Jesus, and He healed them all. It was astonishing. A number of people who were troubled with evil spirits, were set free and everywhere men and women and children gave glory to God, as cripples walked and the blind received their sight. The following morning He was gone! He moved on to the next village, then the next, requiring none to accompany Him, preaching in the synagogues around the Galilee. The four fishermen in Capernaum had no idea what they should do. They wanted to go with him, but they had responsibilities, which needed their attention. Homes and families and businesses made it impossible for them to just up and leave. Sadly, resignedly, they returned to their nets.

For the first time in his life Simon found fishing an anticlimax. Somehow the sea had lost its mystery, the waves no longer exhilarated him and the boat no longer felt like home from home. The challenge of the lake was inept and weak and catching fish seemed rather a futile exercise. It also seemed as though the fish were harder to come by. Suddenly the catch was barely half its original size and, whatever he did to apply his outstanding skills, nothing made the slightest difference. He found himself preoccupied with thoughts of Jesus, about what He might be doing, wishing he was with Him, to watch the people receive hope and healing. Something was happening to Simon bar Jonas. He wanted to fish for men.

It had been a particularly discouraging night. Both pairs of brothers fished from dusk until dawn and caught absolutely nothing. They disembarked, moored the boats and were busily washing out the nets at the side of the lake, when they became aware of a huge crowd, noisily advancing down the grassy slope, which led to the shingle border of the lake. Jesus had returned unexpectedly to Capernaum and was being pursued by crowds of people, who were hungry to hear Him speak and to see the miracles which He did. In their enthusiasm, they were in danger of pushing Jesus into the water. The brothers watched as Jesus waded out towards Simon's boat and hauled Himself aboard. His arms and shoulders were full and strong, from years of physical labour. He called across to Simon and asked him if he would mind manoeuvring the boat a little further away from the land. He did so, then sat in the boat as Jesus used this unlikely pulpit as the stage from which to address the people. He marvelled at the words of love and wisdom which flowed from the compassionate heart of Christ. He saw hope creep into the eyes of the hopeless and despondency yield to joy, as they drank in the words of eternal life. This was fantastic! The boat he had used for years to catch fish was being used to fish for men and Simon knew at that moment, that he wanted to do the same. The time had come for the yoke of service to be laid across the powerful shoulders of Simon bar Jonas, joining him forever to his Lord and thus making him a winner of the souls of men.

The discourse over, the crowd began slowly, somewhat reluctantly, to disperse, and Jesus turned to thank Simon for the use of his boat. Jesus had very little knowledge of the science of fishing. He was an expert with wood, but had never done a day's fishing in His life. Yet He boldly suggested to the experienced fisherman before Him, that he now push his boat out into deeper water and let down his nets for a catch. Simon regarded this amazing man with incredulity. He had laboured long and hard, throughout a night of fruitless fishing. His nets were washed and ready for their next excursion onto the lake and it was completely illogical to expect that he would now catch anything of any significance, especially so close to the shore. Although he had enjoyed listening to Jesus preach to the people and felt privileged to have been of assistance, he suddenly felt extremely tired and just longed for a little sleep. The thought of starting to fish again, catch nothing, and then have to rewash the nets, made him feel sick with lassitude. He offered his protest.

"Master, we have toiled all the night and have taken nothing."

Even as he spoke he knew that he was wrong. He wanted to stop himself, but the words so quickly spilled from his lips. He already knew enough about this man to know that he should never lightly dismiss His words. He recovered himself and, without a pause, continued, "Nevertheless at your word I will let down the net."

And so he did! Assisted by his brother and perhaps remembering the story of how, against logic, the servants at Cana had obeyed Jesus at the wedding feast, he lowered the net into the calm water and immediately felt the increased tension, as they took the weight of a shoal of fish. Those of the crowd who were still tarrying on the beach, watched excitedly as it became obvious that the fishermen had captured a huge quantity of fish. There was a noisy flurry of hurried activity, as the brothers encouraged each other in their efforts to haul the fish on board, and the spectators called their enthusiastic support from the shore, as they watched another obvious miracle.

The net was breaking under the strain and the boat began to tip crazily to starboard. Simon shouted to James and John for help. The two of them were standing like mesmerised spectators, open mouthed at the unprecedented scene that they were witnessing. Simon's call jerked them into action and they rapidly launched the second boat, to cope with the seemingly endless flow of fish. The harvest was so great that both boats were in danger of sinking. In all his years in the fishing industry Simon had never seen the like of this. It was the most astonishing moment of his career. He stood soaking wet on the edge of the lake, gazing with tear filled eyes at the result of his obedience. He looked almost comical, this tough burly man of the sea, with water streaming from his thick curly hair and mingling with the plenteous tears of emotion, which poured like a flood from the fountain of his soul. The power of the moment was overwhelming, the feeling of unworthiness, to be in the presence of the Messiah, the One prophesied to be the deliverer of His people. He turned from the piles of fish and walked humbly to where Jesus was standing. The adoring crowd was pressing closer, but Simon pushed his way through, and in full view of the now silent people, he fell at the feet of the Christ. He was sobbing, but he forced the words through the sobs.

"Depart from me; for I am a sinful man O Lord."

He was not, of course, really asking Him to leave. He felt, in fact, that he never wanted to leave this man from Nazareth for the rest of his life. He was, rather, expressing his unworthiness. He was somewhat frightened by the miracle he had witnessed, but his overwhelming reaction was one of humility. He did not feel worthy to be in the presence of One so great. The Master held out His hand and pulled Simon to his feet.

"Fear not," He said, "from henceforth you will catch men."

It was a special moment in history, the moment which heaven had seen from before the foundations of the world, the moment a man called Simon, an ordinary fisherman, would dedicate his life to become an extraordinary servant of the Son of God. It seemed to Simon that Jesus was saying to him, "Look across your beloved Lake Galilee Simon, this fisherman's plentiful hunting ground, and see the fish which I have just gifted you from its abundant supply. And now lift your spiritual eyes and look across the great ocean of humanity, the sea of souls that I have come to save, and believe that I am able to give you souls from the sea of humankind, as easily as I have provided the fruit of these waters. Follow Me Simon and I will make you a fisher of men."

This time it was for real. This time Simon was giving his all. This time there was no going back. At that moment the lake and its contents ceased to be his life. He was called to catch men for Jesus.

CHAPTER THREE

"Remove from me this hindering flesh;

That I may harvest souls for Thee;

Eliminate polluting dross;

But give me strength to bear my cross"

SIMON PETER SOON BEGAN TO realise that the transformation from fisherman to fisher of men was not an overnight miracle. It was going to take time. He did, at first, have huge, even world changing expectations of his new found vocation, but he quickly realised, that those who aspire to change the world, must themselves first be changed. As he listened to the words of Jesus and began to observe the way that He lived, he understood that even He was not an independent entity. He relied completely on His Father for everything which He both said and did, so that the words which He spoke and the miracles which He performed, were not His own, but His Fathers. His only power was that which He received from His communion with God. His commitment was to do His Father's will, rather than His own and that required Him to be in constant fellowship with His Father for both guidance, direction and power. It also necessitated the maintaining of the highest level of self discipline, at all times refusing to yield to the tempting of His flesh and, rising to every succeeding challenge, grow constantly and consistently in spiritual strength and character. Peter saw that even Jesus needed to learn obedience, by the things which He suffered in everyday life. The discipline of adversity was working in Him the ability to conquer future obstacles, each act of obedience requiring a new level of commitment. Peter sensed that his mentor was enduring a process which was making Him complete in every experience of life, bringing Him inexorably to His ultimate destiny. Peter was right. He knew nothing of the true destination of the Man he followed, but the fact was that Jesus was not yet ready to arrive, because He was not yet fully prepared. He was eventually laid upon the cross at thirty three years of age because it took that period of time to prepare for it. A year earlier He was not ready and would have failed. The process which Peter observed unfolding in the life of the Messiah, was the pattern which his own life must follow. It was necessary for him to "Follow Me" before he could be a "fisher of men." When Jesus called him to "follow" He meant far more than the obvious. He meant that he must walk the same road of preparation for service, which would be the changing room, from which would eventually emerge a "fisher of men."

Peter was a practical man, renowned for his impetuous and outspoken disposition, which has come to be universally regarded as an almost endearing flaw in his character, although, as far as God was concerned, it was a temperament much in need of reining in and channelling correctly. Jesus had only three, short years to subject this man to the discipline which was necessary for his metamorphosis from fisherman to fisher of men. Without it, he would drown in the first storm upon the great sea of human need. Peter knew enough of the history of his people to know that the same principles of preparation and discipline were applied to men like Abraham, Moses, Joshua, and even the great King David. They and countless others endured the purging of suffering, before they became truly effective. If Peter was to leave his mark upon the world and fulfil the Divine purpose for his life, then he also must experience the chastisement of his flesh. There is no shortcut to such development. The responsibility of his calling was underlined on the morning that Jesus announced the names of His twelve apostles, ones chosen from the main body of disciples, to be the foundation stones and leaders of the church which He had come to produce. Typically, Jesus did not make the choice Himself, but spent the entire night in the seclusion of the mountain in communion with His Father. There, Father and Son talked together about the future and Jesus emerged with the names His Father gave to Him. First, and unquestionably their leader, was Simon Peter, followed by his brother Andrew and the two sons of Zebedee. Then came Philip and Bartholomew, Matthew, Thomas, James the son of Alpheus, Simon Zelotes, Judas the brother of James (sometimes called Thaddeus or Lebbeus and author of the book of Jude) and finally, Judas Iscariot. The importance of these ministries and the responsibility they carried cannot be overstressed and was attested on that amazing day of ordination, by an extraordinary display of God's power upon the people who waited at the foot of the hill for the descent of the Christ. They came from Jerusalem and Judea, from the sea coasts of Tyre and Sidon and from all the regions of Galilee, all wanting to see, or if possible, to touch, the Son of God. Many did touch Him, most of them sick, many of them dying, and virtue went out from Him and healed them all.

Peter stood with the others and watched the Master at work. Love and compassion flowed from His hands and diseases shrank and withered at his touch. Cripples walked, the blind received their sight, dumb lips shouted for joy, and the multitude sang hymns of praise to the God of Israel. He knew that he was called to represent this amazing man and he felt so completely unequipped. Never in the history of the world had mortal man been entrusted with the kind of power and responsibility, which was being thrust upon him and his fellow apostles. To suggest that they, or any others, could embark upon this supernatural mission, without serious discipline and preparation, was ludicrous and would be a denial of the very pattern and process which was applied to Jesus Himself. Peter knew, as he bathed in the emotional high of that morning of miracles, that there could be no fruit without first breaking up the ground, no resurrection power without suffering, no crown without a cross, no glory without tears and no rejoicing without pain. He who was called to be a central part of God's universal plan, must be refashioned for the job. His character must be moulded and perfected in the crucible of affliction, testing and tempering him for the work ahead. He knew that without it he would never survive. He would become a victim of his own fleshly weaknesses and probably be destroyed by his inherent impetuosity. Peter did not need an out-of-balance view of the character of God, portraying Him as all love and sweetness at the expense of righteousness, purity and justice. Three critical years lay ahead of him, which must see him broken and placed once more on the wheel of the Great Potter.

So it was that the dealings of Jesus with His fisherman friend were often far from pleasant. He was allowed to get away with nothing. He was challenged about every reaction, every attitude, and every motive. It often seemed as though Jesus was being pedantic, even rude, in His dealings with His disciple, but it was for a higher purpose. And He expected him to learn quickly. Time was at a premium for both teacher and pupil. This was clearly illustrated on the occasion when Jesus was teaching the multitudes concerning that which defiles a man being more to do with the condition of the heart, than with the contents of his belly. When Peter approached Jesus later in the day to ask for clarification of the meaning, he received a stern rebuke.

"Are you also without understanding?"

Initially Peter thought that the words of Jesus were somewhat harsh, but as he lay that night under a bright moonlit sky, trying not to feel sorry for himself, he acknowledged that Jesus obviously expected better of him. He should have been more alert and focussed during the discourse, more keen to grasp and remember truth. Basically, Jesus was right, he should have understood.

The weeks became months and, with the passing of time, increased revelation brought more responsibility. Several times Peter found himself on the receiving end of comments like "Oh ye of little faith" or "Where is your faith?" Tell-tale glances of disapproval, times when Jesus seemed to ignore him, all served to press home lessons which were essential for the future. There was the time when Jesus was attempting to warn them concerning His approaching death and resurrection, when Peter presumed to take his Master aside and reprove Him for, what seemed to him, to be negative and defeatist words. Nobody can doubt his sincerity and motivation, for he loved Jesus with deep devotion and was understandably appalled at the suggestion that He might die. Such an idea certainly did not dovetail into his perceived pattern for the future and he obviously believed that Jesus was wrong to even speak of such matters. The fact was, however, that he was seriously lacking in spiritual perception and, notwithstanding the purity of his motives, received the strongest and most painful rebuke of his life. Jesus looked at him with those piercing, penetrating eyes, which appeared on fire with disproportionate indignation.

"Get thee behind me Satan: thou art an offence unto me: for thou savourest not the things that be of God, but those that be of men."

Peter's face flushed deep red with resentment, hurt and embarrassment. He wanted to retaliate, to defend himself, to challenge the righteousness of such cruel words. He knew that he sometimes spoke when silence was a wiser option, but he could see no justification for this! To be called Satan was surely a step too far. He considered himself to be his Lord's must loyal and trusted friend, for whom he had forsaken everything, and now he was rewarded by being called by the name of the prince of darkness. The words stung him to his core. He didn't know whether to cry or be angry, to stand and fight his cause, or walk away in disgust. He slowly turned and with tears stinging his eyes, walked away from the group. He wanted to be alone, to ask God why he seemed to always be treated like an enemy, instead of a friend.

Peter was absent for a long time. He found that his sense of hurt and self pity was an obstacle to clear thinking. It was difficult to remove the caustic words of Jesus from his mind, because he felt that he did not even begin to deserve them. He tried to look for a reason, but his mind shouted the words at him, "Get thee behind me Satan", and the words gave no space for reason. He sat alone and held his head in his hands, seeking to look past his resentment and listen to the voice of God. It took a while, but eventually he began to see the possible seriousness of what he had done. It seemed preposterous, but if by some strange providence, Almighty God was intent on accomplishing His purposes through the death of His Son, then he could see that for him to so dogmatically oppose the plan, was, in a way, doing the work of Satan, who was, of course, committed to contest any and every plan of God. He could not begin to understand why, or how, Jesus should die, but he decided that in future he would not argue with anything that He said. He concluded that he must acknowledge, that however right he might believe himself to be, he could be wrong, and that, however good and pure his motives might be, they never justified error. He also learned that a good heart and expressions of love and care, unless matured in the womb of wisdom, can become the tools of evil. He learned that the finest of lines separated the passion of the human spirit from the guidance of the Holy Spirit and that the worlds on either side of that line can be as diverse as God and Satan. These were massive lessons, which he would never forget, because of the searing power of the words used in the rebuke. Had the correction been clothed in niceties and gentility, the lesson might have been forgotten, but, as Peter returned to take his place in the group, he knew that this was a day that he would never forget.

Only six days after the "Get thee behind me Satan" rebuke, Peter was invited by the Lord Jesus to accompany Him and James and John, on one of His visits into the mountain for a time of prayer. It was not unusual for the disciples to see Jesus disappearing into some convenient hillside for a secret meeting with His Father. He would often be gone all night, to reappear at dawn with His face radiant with the glory of another world and His spirit energised with healing virtue, with which He healed the constant flow of sick people, who came to Him for help. Peter was relieved to be included. It confirmed his reinstatement to favour after the rebuke of the previous week.

It was warm and humid. The only sound was the song of a lone nightingale, adding its sweet sound to the ambiance of the night. The stars flickered silently against the dark cushion of the heavens and within minutes Peter was struggling to remain conscious. He tried to pray, but his mind wandered, out of control, in a vortex of mundane and unproductive thoughts, which inevitably sucked him into the world of sleep. He slept peacefully, as did his two friends. Only Jesus cast off weariness and sought the presence of God in prayer.

Peter dreamed that he was out fishing on the lake. It was noontime and the sun was at its zenith, hot and unrelenting. The brightness of the sun was reflecting from the surface of the water and blinding his eyes. He shaded his face with his hands and narrowed his eyes to find focus in the glare of moving light. It seemed surreal. The light was beyond anything he had experienced before. It was as though he was sailing in an orb of blazing, unbearable glory. Suddenly he was awake, but the light in his dream was still with him. He was not sure whether he was awake or asleep, for the light was blinding his eyes. He turned and looked back towards the plain and there was only darkness, but the mountain was ablaze with glory. Jesus stood in its centre and with Him two strangers. They had obviously been in serious conversation for some time and somehow, he had no idea how, Peter recognised them as men from the past. One was Moses, the great lawgiver and deliverer of Israel, and the other was Elijah, the figurehead of all Old Testament prophets. They were present as two men who had both ended their earthly service prematurely, but were now afforded the opportunity of encouraging Jesus in the decease He was to accomplish at Jerusalem. The law and the prophets were combining to inspire the beginning of the dispensation of grace. Peter, James and John were given the privilege of being privy to this amazing and historic conversation, but they missed it because they slept, when they should have prayed.

He gazed with awe at the One who had called him from the fishing nets. He was no longer an average looking Jewish male. He was standing in another realm, the King of another Kingdom. His entire being was transfigured, His countenance shining like the brightness of the noonday sun, and His clothes were flashing and glowing with a supernatural light. It was awesome, overwhelming, frightening! It was many years later that Peter realised that this night on the mountain was, in fact, a preview of the second advent of the Christ, when, at the close of time, He will come to reign. As an elderly man in Rome, he referred to this astonishing night and wrote in a letter to the churches, "We were eyewitnesses of His majesty."

Peter's fear gave way to excitement, and excitement to irrational and presumptuous conclusions. He and his companions believed that Jesus was the Messiah, but their expectation was that he would drive the Roman oppressors from the land and set up His Great Kingdom here and now, re-establishing the royal line of David. Surely this was it! They were gazing upon the King in all His glory. On the same day that Jesus had rebuked Peter six days before, He had told them that some of them would see the Son of Man coming in His Kingdom. The presence of the great prophet Elijah was another sign, for the prophet Malachi declared that Elijah would come before the great and terrible day of the Lord. It all made sense! The Kingdom had come at last! How soon Peter had forgotten the conversation about Jesus dying, which had spawned the painful rebuke of the previous week. He chose to remember that which related to glory, but neglected that which indicated death, even though the conversations took place on the same day. He was all too ready to grab for the crown and forget the cross. The fact was that, if he had not slept when Jesus asked him to pray, he would have heard Moses and Elijah speaking with Jesus about His coming death in Jerusalem, and he would not have made the mistake and placed himself once more on the receiving end of another rebuke. If he had thought back six days, he would have remembered Jesus talking about self denial and carrying a cross, but instead he wanted to prolong the glory. He wanted to cling to this supernatural manifestation and live inside it forever. His excitement stirred his impetuosity and flesh dared to speak in the presence of the Divine.

"Lord, it is good for us to be here: if thou wilt, let us make here three tabernacles; one for thee, and one for Moses, and one for Elias."

The rebuke was instant, before the words were out of his mouth, and more frightening than any of them had ever experienced before. In seconds, the mountain was shrouded in a thick, white, blinding mist. Peter could see nothing. Then, out of the cloud, crashing like thunder against his terrified life, came the voice of Almighty God.

"This is My beloved Son, in Whom I am well pleased, hear ye Him."

The words, "Hear ye Him" were pronounced, indignant and commanding. Peter was afraid. He fell on his face before the glory of the Creator. He knew that once more he had spoken unadvisedly and this time He had invoked the wrath of God. How dreadful was this holy mount. How foolish was this unlearned fisherman and how slow to learn. He dared not even lift his face. He remained with his eyes closed and his face buried in the dust of the hill. He did not move until he felt a gentle touch upon his shoulder, whereupon he raised his head and saw the Saviour standing before him. Moses and Elijah were no longer there, only Jesus, standing in the ethereal aftermath of the glory, which still lingered on His garments, His eyes full of love and pity for His erring servant. The lesson of a week before was reaffirmed and new ones added. Sleep is the thief of prayer and revelation, glory is not always for now and is usually preceded by suffering, and euphoria, emotion and excitement are often the breeding ground for hasty words and presumptuous acts. It was a shamefaced and humbled Peter who descended the mountain to begin another day of service.

So the transformation of Peter continued, by teaching and rebuke, by example and correction, slowly the Great Teacher moulded His servant of clay into a rock upon which He could build. It appeared sometimes as though Peter needed more discipline than his peers, not because he was any worse than them, but because each individual has a particular path to tread and God knows best how to prepare each one for his calling. There were undoubtedly times when Jesus targeted Peter for rebuke, when others were equally guilty; like that sombre hour in the Garden of Gethsemane, when the same three apostles once more fell asleep, when they were asked to pray. All three were guilty, but it was Peter who He held to account.

"And He cometh to His disciples, and findeth them asleep, and saith unto Peter, What, could you not watch with me one hour?"

Peter once again felt an inclination to resentment and the desire to indulge in self pity, but he had learned by now to trust the wisdom and the fairness of his Lord. Whatever the other two had done, he knew that he was guilty. He must once more learn the lesson and go on. Unfortunately, as a direct result of his indolence, he once again fell a prey to his impetuosity, not this time with a verbal outburst, but with an act of violence. He was jolted from sleep by the arrival of Judas Iscariot and the mob that had come to arrest Jesus. In an instant he drew his sword and took a swing at the head of the high priest's servant, Malchus, narrowly missing cleaving him down the middle, but lopping off his ear. Maybe he thought, in the heat of the moment, that his loyal defence of his Lord would bring him a commendation, but instead it produced yet another rebuke.

"Put up again thy sword into his place: for all they that take the sword shall perish with the sword. Thinkest thou that I cannot now pray the Father, and He shall presently give me more than twelve legions of angels?"

Peter turned away in remorse, watching helplessly, as his best friend was led away like an animal down the slope of Olivet, to the valley below. He had done it again. Mistake after mistake seemed to be his destiny. At that moment he wanted to quit, go back to fishing the lake and just accept that he would never make it. Or perhaps tomorrow would be a better day? But tomorrow was going to be the worst day of his entire life. Tomorrow was to go down in history as the day of Simon Peter's biggest mistake. Tomorrow, the lovable fisherman was going to hit rock bottom. "Follow Me", Jesus had said, "and I will make you fishers of men." Peter was beginning to understand what those words really meant, as he experienced the pain of the sharp cutting tools, which the spiritual carpenter, who was employed to make him the complete fisherman, must apply to his life. They were always grievous, never pleasant, for, in the Master's hand, they cut away the raw flesh of an unworthy Galilean, in order to produce the peaceable fruit of righteousness.

CHAPTER FOUR

"Oh Master let me walk with Thee,
Where none have ever walked before;
Transcending laws of natural earth,
On ocean deep bring faith to birth"

THE THREE YEARS OR MORE which Peter spent in the company and service of Jesus of Nazareth, was not a continuous and unending saga of failure and discipline. It often seemed like that to Peter, like the briefest nightmare often appears to consume a whole night of sleep, but the fact is that they were years of joy, laughter and adventure, as a developing faith took him into a realm beyond the natural, allowing him to taste the power of God beyond his dreams and preparing him to minister into the lives of multitudes. He learned to obey his Lord even in the preposterous, but he always proved it to be the best. Like the day that Jesus challenged him to cast a line into the sea when they needed money to pay their taxes and he found a coin in the fish's mouth. Or the time he was involved in handing out five small bread rolls and two fishes to a crowd numbering many thousands, and then watched the food multiply before his eyes until everyone was amply fed and twelve baskets of leftovers were collected. This and much, much more served to feed the faith and development of

Simon Peter. There was no wonder that the people were mindful to take Jesus and forcibly make Him their king. Such an absolute sensation as this, not only aroused popular enthusiasm amongst the people, but spurred the apostles to believe all the more for the exaltation of their Master to the throne of David.

The sun was low on the horizon as the people dispersed on that amazing evening of the feeding of the five thousand men plus women and children. The surface of the Sea of Galilee had already lost the light and a foreboding restlessness moved across the darkening waters as the wind freshened from the east. Peter stood at the edge of the water and smiled grimly at his old friend and enemy. He knew the signs. He had experienced this lake from childhood. The wind would increase until it howled down every wadi between both northern and eastern hills, turning the lake into a boiling cauldron of angry waves. This was certainly not going to be a night for sea travel. He turned as he heard the voice of Jesus behind him.

"Peter, if you and the others take the boat and head for Bethsaida, I will remain here until all the people have gone and then spend a while in prayer in the mountain."

Peter hesitated before replying, "Master, the weather is turning. It is not wise for us to cross the lake the way things are."

Jesus looked at him, like a father looks at a naive child who fails to obey instructions. He held his eyes with His own, reminding him without words of the morning on the beach, when Peter thought it was foolish to cast the nets after a night of fruitless fishing. It turned out to be the most amazing morning of Peter's life. A faint smile edged the older man's lips.

"Whatever you say, Master, whatever you say."

Darkness was closing in on Lake Galilee as they rowed out into the deep and in less than half an hour Peter's worst fears were realised. The storm rose like a monster from the belly of the sea, sudden and violent. Scattered clouds scurried across the face of the rising moon and the temperature dropped alarmingly as the warm air on the surface of the lake sucked in the cold winds from the hills of Hermon. The small craft became a stranded victim in the centre of the storm and was soon sliding from each rising wave into the watery valley between it and the next. The oars were largely ineffective against the powers of nature and as a result the ship was rudderless, often spinning out of control at the mercy of the elements. Despite the best efforts of these experienced and talented seamen, they were making no actual progress in crossing the lake. Meanwhile, from His mountain vantage point of prayer, Jesus searched the wild darkness of the lake, occasionally catching a glimpse of the tiny boat, and its precious cargo, in the frequent bursts of moonlight. His friends were obviously toiling without effect against the contrary wind.

They fought for hours, until exhaustion overwhelmed them. Every muscle ached under the strain and their eyes stung with the lashing of wind and water. This was not the first time that Peter had fought the elements on Lake Galilee, but by the beginning of the fourth watch of the night he was experiencing the hopelessness felt only by the utterly weary. He feared for their lives. It was now 3am and they had travelled only half of the six-mile crossing.

Soon their meagre efforts would yield to the unabated strength of the storm and they would be sucked beneath the hungry waters to their deaths. Peter indulged himself in a pensive backward glance to the shore, which they had left so many hours before. He could see, beyond the rising bank which ran up and away towards the mountain range beyond, spasmodically silhouetted against the moonlit sky and the fast moving clouds, the hill, where he knew was the man, who, only hours before, had miraculously fed the multitudes. Now they needed Him and He was nowhere to be seen. He could not understand it. Why had He insisted that they make this crazy journey? They were only on the lake because they were being obedient to the One whom they had promised to follow. Were they now going to die because they had obeyed His voice? Surely they could not perish on a journey orchestrated by the Christ?

A wave crashed over the boat and he knew that they were in imminent danger of sinking. Fear tightened his chest as he watched his companions cling to anything they could wrap their arms around. They slipped into survival mode. He heard his friend John crying out to the God of Abraham, that their lives might be spared. It was then, beyond the desperate figure of his fearing friend, that Peter thought he saw something moving on the water. He tried to focus on the area in question and searched the darkness, but the boat spun and he lost his bearings. The moon was eclipsed with heavy cloud and the spray from the hissing sea was kicking high and filling the wind with mist. He continued to stare into the swirling darkness. He was sure that he had seen something. He began to turn away, but, as he did so, it was there again, emerging from the spray and riding the waves with kingly dignity. It was the ghostly silhouette of a man. Then it was gone, hidden once more behind a towering wave and swallowed by the relentless ferocity of the gale. Peter's heart pounded with a mixture of fear and exhilaration. He shouted to the others and pointed, but as they turned the vision was no more. Still he urged them to look and they searched the turbulent scene as one. There it was again! Closer now! Little more than three ships lengths away! The figure was striding from wave to wave, undaunted by the lashing spray, his garments blowing in the wind, the emblem of celestial majesty. Someone cried out with fear, believing that some ghostly apparition, some evil spirit of the lake, had come to claim its victims and so seal their fate. Surely, there was significance in this vision of the supernatural, some threatening prediction of impending doom. Yet as the men cried out with fear, a voice of serene authority rose above the cacophony of the storm.

"Be of good cheer; it is I; be not afraid."

Peter instantaneously experienced a surge of overwhelming relief, which was then immediately replaced with waves of wonderment. His fear disappeared in an instant and tears of gratitude flowed from his tired eyes. His circumstances were the same. The storm still pounded their frail vessel, but he suddenly felt safe. What manner of man was this Jesus of Nazareth that He could walk with such calmness across the raging sea? Was nothing beyond the supernatural ability of this humble carpenter's son? How wrong he was to ever doubt His word, or suspect that He could fail, or forsake them, in times of danger. How he loved Him! At that moment Peter wanted nothing more than to be with his Lord, to know Him where He was, to walk with Him in His kingly realm, to feel what He felt, to breathe the same breath of heaven that He breathed. He suddenly felt an urge to leap from the tortured ship and walk those proud and angry waves with his Lord. And then, just like the morning at Bethabara and the day on the beach at Capernaum, Jesus began to walk away (iv). To Peter's amazement and chagrin, He was now heading away from their boat. Peter could not believe his eyes and he lifted his hands in horror. The Peter of old would have followed his instinct and desire and impetuously leaped from the ship, but he had learned something from the discipline he had received. Despite the indisputable fact that the initiative to walk on the water with Jesus came from Peter, the boldness of his natural spirit, if applied to this situation, would have undoubtedly meant certain death. To join the Master on the tempestuous sea needed more than emotional fervour, or the passion of sincerity. Human beings cannot walk on water, but they can walk upon the word of the Almighty. He needed a word of command from the One who rules the wind and waters. With that, in obedience to that, he could do anything. So, having conceived the notion, he asked for the word from which true faith is born.

"Lord, if it be Thou, bid me come to Thee on the water."

He shouted it above the noise of the wind and the crashing of the waves. He was not questioning the identity of the man who walked the water. He was inviting the Son of God to challenge him, to speak a word upon which he could place his trust and confidence. Immediately the Saviour turned and faced the boat and His voice issued the required command.

"Come," was all that the Master said. Just one word! Peter needed no great oration. One word from the lips of Jesus was enough. Peter asked for a word from the One who, by a word, called the worlds into being, and the single word, "come" was all that he needed. In an instant, to the horror of his colleagues, he was climbing onto the side of the pitching boat and looked as though he would be swept to his death in the angry sea. He paused, only for a moment and then stepped calmly onto the next wave. In a second it carried him on its moving belly, away from the ship, but miraculously bore his weight. Peter laughed uproariously, as he strode from wave to wave. He picked his way across the moving floor of water towards his Lord. Their eyes met through the mist and Jesus smiled at His faithful friend. He would go far, this bold and impetuous Jew.

Only for a second Peter looked down at the waves. He felt the power of the wind and feared that it would blow him off course. He simply glanced down in order to steady himself, but as he looked into the darkness of the boiling water at his feet, panic seized his legs and faith surrendered to logic. He began to sink! In one brief moment of doubt he stepped out of the supernatural, back into the natural world. He lost sight of the word he had received and natural reason overcame his mind.

"Lord, save me," he yelled.

He immediately felt the strong arm of Jesus grip his own, lifting him up and steadying him once more upon the sea of faith. Then, not prepared to miss the opportunity of giving another lesson in this most unlikely classroom, Jesus chided with him, as a father scolds a son.

"O thou of little faith, wherefore didst thou doubt."

Then they were striding the waves together, hand in hand, the Creator and His creation, the Teacher and His pupil. The wind was still boisterous, the tempest still raged, the boat was pitching violently, but Peter laughed at it all, because he was walking with Jesus. He knew that once more he had failed, by looking at the problem instead of keeping his eyes on Jesus, but what a lesson to learn! And at least he had got out of the boat! Maybe in future years, people would criticise him for beginning to sink, but he didn't care. He was walking the stormy waters with his Lord, and not many others in history would ever do that.

Peter had a cold and wet body, but a glowing heart, as they arrived back, the fisherman and his Lord, at the distressed ship and its astonished seafarers. As they climbed on board the wind ceased and the lake became calm, instantly subdued by the mighty hand of the Almighty. And they came, each man on board, and knelt at the feet of the Master and worshipped Him.

"Of a truth," they said, "thou art the Son of God."

Peter did not know it, but his initiative to do what he saw Jesus doing that night, not only saved the lives of his fellow servants on board the ship, but the millions of souls who were destined to become a part of the universal church of Jesus Christ across the centuries, through their witness. The whole investment of Christ on earth, the foundation stones for the building of His Kingdom, was in that boat. Peter's faith, albeit flawed, could have actually saved the future of the church.

CHAPTER FIVE

"Let soul and mind both shaken be,
'Till hell becomes an end deserved;
Let failure steal his final breath
And faith sink hapless into death"

IN THE DARK WORLD OF the demonic, where good is evil and evil good, where purity is filth and debauchery is honoured, where love is despised and hatred extolled; in the nucleus of darkness, which is the cesspit of evil, from which flows the pollution which brings misery and death to humankind, here, in the caverns of hell, Satan himself rules over his hoards of evil intelligentsia. He is not omnipresent, but through an organised structure of intelligent, evil spiritual powers, is fully conversant with the happenings on planet earth, taking particular notice of those who, by reason of their commitment to love and serve Jesus Christ, are his sworn enemies. He is constantly updated by principalities and powers which rule over nations, cities, towns and communities, they being informed by an organised structure of demonic hierarchy of greater and lesser demons, concerning the activities of those who threaten his kingdom with the power of the Gospel.

Satan had long been aware of the identity of the One known as Jesus of Nazareth and of those He had chosen to be His apostles, taking particular note of the one to whom Jesus had said, "Thou art Peter, and upon this rock I will build My church and the gates of hell shall not prevail against it. And I will give to thee the keys of the kingdom." This man was recognised in the world of the demonic as an individual of significant threat, a warrior of the hated kingdom of heaven, with the ability to bind and liberate according to the Divine purpose. He was marked as a potential thorn in the side of Satan, a puller-down of the strongholds of evil, an invader of the citadels of darkness, a plunderer of devilish domains, and a liberator of the people through his fearless preaching of the Gospel. He was therefore designated for destruction. He must not be allowed to reach maturity as a selfless servant of Jesus.

News of the amazing demonstration of faith displayed by Peter, in his act of walking on the Sea of Galilee, did nothing to allay the fear of the threat that this man posed to the world of evil. Agitated chatter between high ranking demons resulted in application for help being submitted to the prince of darkness himself. God's attention to justice was well known to His enemies and had been used to possible advantage in the past. The satanic realm was fully aware of certain divine principles which were set in stone. For example it was obvious that, in the despised kingdom of light, increased revelation requires a proportionate increase in responsibility and that the bestowing of divine favour is expected to produce deeper levels of faithfulness. Satan had used this to some effect, in requesting access to God's servant Job, thousands of years before. It was obvious that this man, Peter, had been singled out for special treatment and called to high office in the hated kingdom of the Christ, so should he not, in justice, be put to the test? Satan decided to make application for protection to be removed from this despicable sea-walker and that permission be granted for a full scale attack to be launched against him. God had declared him to be a rock! Let the rock now be put to the test!

So it was that, on the evening of the Last Supper, before He departed for the Garden of Gethsemane, Jesus took Peter aside to speak with him privately. There was no harshness in the Saviour's tone, no hint of rebuke or condemnation, only an earnest, deep-felt concern for his welfare. He used his old name, for it was to his old weaknesses that his enemy would apply the pressure. And He repeated his name, as an expression of the depth of His concern.

"Simon, Simon, behold, Satan hath desired to have you, that he may sift you as wheat: but I have prayed for thee that thy faith fail not: and when thou art converted, strengthen thy brethren."

Each word was pronounced with passion, pleading for Peter's attention at the deepest level. Jesus gripped both his hands and looked with undisguised concern into the eyes of His servant. He wanted him to listen. He must not treat this warning lightly. It was as though Jesus had overheard the demand of the vile accuser and had discerned the ferocity of the hatred that he felt for Peter. He was pleading for Peter to prepare for the biggest test of his life. He knew that, despite the many hard lessons which the fisherman had learned over the last three years, he still had numerous faults, each of which made him vulnerable to his enemy. He knew that Satan would not attack his strengths, but his weaknesses, and that he would stop at nothing to bring him down (v).

It is possible that Satan had accused Peter, before God, of being false, a follower of Jesus for what he could get out of it for himself. Although this was clearly untrue, the disciples had certainly shown themselves capable of misguided motives, even arguing amongst themselves who would be the greatest in the coming kingdom. Now Satan demanded that Peter's sincerity and loyalty be put to the test. He wanted licence to 'sift' Peter like wheat, to violently shake him, in an attempt to prove that he would fail under pressure and be proved to be nothing but chaff blowing in the wind, a servant unworthy of his calling.

Peter was given the privilege of both warning and encouragement in the words of the Lord Jesus. It was an amazing act of selfless love that the Master should seek to so passionately minister to another, at the time when the oppression and foreboding of His own imminent death, was pressing in upon Him. Yet Peter seemed naively oblivious to the seriousness of the hour. He was being warned of supernatural conflict, but at the same time was assured that the Son of God had made personal intercession that his faith should not fail in the fight, yet neither seemed to have the impact that was needful. It would have been prudent of Peter to humbly thank his Lord for His counsel and prayers, with a sombre and appreciative spirit, or perhaps to have asked advice about what he could do to prepare his heart for the pending conflict. Instead, he acted the part of the old Simon with typical outspoken confidence.

"Lord, I am ready to go with Thee, both into prison, and to death."

There is no doubt that Peter believed that he meant his rash declaration. He really did think that he loved this "Son of the living God" enough to die for Him, but he was wrong. He was oblivious to his own weakness and cowardice. He could not possibly know how he would act in circumstances which he had never engaged. He thought he knew and it was good for him to pray that, if tested to the ultimate, he would remain faithful and courageous, but it was dangerous and unacceptable to so boldly predict his future conduct. It was a massive mistake. The one, who so often had unadvisedly opened his mouth without wisdom, now did so in the face of satanic opposition. His words were his enemy's ideal opportunity and therefore, the harbinger of Peter's downfall. He was no longer a novice. He had received correction on numerous occasions concerning the danger of rash words. Satan had the right to demand that he now be tested on his latest claim. Peter's confident assertion gave his enemy his target and his weapon, and the hordes of hell moved in to engulf the mind of the unsuspecting Galilean.

It was past midnight when the group of young men left the scene of the last supper and headed towards the Kidron valley. The Lord Jesus had done his absolute best to prepare His followers for the dark hours that lay ahead of them. That night, in an extended discourse in the upper room, he promised them "another comforter" in the person of the Holy Spirit. He encouraged them to focus their attention on the eternal world and upon the place that He was going to prepare for them. He then prayed for them with heart-felt passion, before leading them in the singing of a psalm. They crossed the ravine and began the slow ascent to the Mount of Olives. The sense of melancholy, disquiet and apprehension, which they all felt in the upper room, now closed in on them like a suffocating mist and Jesus was visibly troubled. He was concerned for all of them, but especially for Peter. He had been far too quick to dismiss His warning about Satan's plan and the Master feared for His servant. He decided to broach the subject again in more general terms. Without addressing His words to any particular individual He said, "All ye shall be offended because of Me this night; for it is written, I will smite the shepherd, and the sheep shall be scattered."

It was a still, silent night and the bold voice of Peter resonated through the uncanny darkness of the mount.

"Although all shall be offended, yet will not I."

Jesus winced with horror at the rash words of His friend. Would he never learn the wisdom of a still tongue? In just a few minutes they would enter the garden called Gethsemane and He knew that He would then be engaged in a personal struggle, which would require His complete attention and drain away His last drop of energy. Soon Peter must fight alone and it was obvious that he was ill-prepared, still confident in himself and completely unaware that he was prone to fail. In the presence of them all, Jesus rebuked Peter with prophetic words that were designed to jolt him into realising his own vulnerability.

"Verily I say unto thee, that this day, even in this night, before the cock crow twice, thou shalt deny Me thrice."

His words bounced off Peter without effect. They failed to break his natural spirit. There was no inner hearkening to the Lord's caring words of warning. Instead, defying caution and with a complete absence of discernment, he answered with reckless passion, "If I should die with Thee, I will not deny Thee in any wise." An expression of unutterable sadness clouded the eyes of Jesus.

Then they were there, at the garden called Gethsemane, the ordained battle ground for both Master and servant. A strange atmosphere, a silence which could be felt, shrouded the garden and a ghostly moonlight cast unnerving shadows between the twisted olive trees. Beneath them lay the city of Jerusalem, asleep, while the Son of God, who had wept over her future from this very hillside, now knelt in the agony of intercession. He did not want to die. He certainly did not deserve to die. Yet He knew that He was here for that purpose. Sin demanded death for its guilty victims and he was the only one qualified, by a sinless life, to pay the price. He was facing the most gruesome death imaginable, which included bearing upon His spotless and blameless person, the filth and sin of the entire human race. He knew that it was the Father's will that He pay the price in full, but He also knew that it had to be a willing sacrifice, and His pure being shrank from the cup of universal sin and suffering which was being proffered to His lips. He took Peter, James and John, deep into an enclave of trees at the nether end of the garden. He asked them to pray with Him, whilst He went a little further and knelt alone in the moonlight.

Peter's mind was blitzed with thoughts of doubt and death and fear. He engaged the world of supernatural mental combat and his natural confidence fled like husks before the wind. He knelt to pray at the request of his Lord, to support Him in His hour of greatest need, but found that he was weak in the face of overwhelming satanic force. His mind became the playground for negative thoughts. A demonic heaviness fell over him like a thick blanket and swirling darkness and the hideous images of demons, their faces contorted with hatred and evil, zoomed in and out on the screen of his mind. A feeling of abject despair inexplicably swamped his spirit and his will to fight was lost in weariness.

He yielded to sleep, but it was the restless sleep of a defeated man.

He was roused from sleep by yet another rebuke from Jesus. His Lord was displeased that he had gone to sleep in the hour of crisis. Jesus did not expect less from him because the hour was difficult; indeed it was for times of crisis that he had been trained and more was required of him now, than ever before. To sleep in the face of the enemy, in the hour of battle, was the epitome of folly. The fisherman's soul was in jeopardy and he needed to pray. Unfortunately he did not. Despite the rebuke, He slept on. While Jesus, involved in a far greater battle, triumphed in prayer by the genuine surrender of His will to the will of His Father, His servant succumbed to the powers of darkness. For Peter, Gethsemane became the garden of defeat. The sifting process had begun and the sifter of souls already had the advantage. He was already weakened by the first salvo from hell. His flesh was strong, but his spirit was weak and only a resolute spirit was capable of seeing him through the perilous waters which lay ahead of him. Peter was heading for a fall.

Suddenly they were upon them. Judas Iscariot, one of the twelve, with Malchus, servant of the high priest, numerous other members of the Sanhedrin police force, and a band of Roman soldiers. They were there to arrest Jesus. When the mob finally led their prisoner from the garden, tethered around the neck like an animal, Peter followed at a distance, still a free man. But in the spiritual realm the bound man was free, His ship on course for victory. It was the physically free man who was destined for defeat, his frail boat heading for the rocks.

CHAPTER SIX

"Oh dark betrayal of my dearest friend;
Dread cowardice that came between;
No measure of heartfelt remorse,
Can my deep penitence endorse"

THE NIGHT AIR WAS DAMP and cold as the group left the Garden of Gethsemane, a place now forever marked with the aura of a sacred moment in history, and made its way down the moonlit Olivet. The Roman tribune had, cruelly and quite unnecessarily, ordered that the hands of Jesus be bound behind His back and that a rope be tied around His neck, with which to lead Him. As a consequence He found some difficulty in negotiating the uneven pathway which led down to the Kidron ravine and then across and up to the impressive palace of the high priest, home to both Annas and his son-in-law, Caiaphas. Peter followed at a safe distance. John, the son of Zebedee, remained with the group. The rest of the disciples had fled, for fear of their lives.

John, who was acquainted with the high priest and his family, was allowed into the building where Jesus was to appear before Annas. Initially, Peter was left out in the street, but after some persuasion by his friend John, the young woman who kept the door finally granted him access. He was shown into an open courtyard which was the centre of Caiaphas' luxurious dwelling. The house was complete with every possible amenity, including ritual pools and extravagant furnishings. It had everything necessary to provide a lavish lifestyle for the priests. The rooms were built around the courtyard, and it was here that a nervous looking Peter found a seat close to the open fire. He had a full view of Jesus, who was in front of him in the judgement hall. Behind him, was the arched entrance to the porch area, and beyond that, the main exit to the street.

Simon Peter was confused and bewildered. It wasn't supposed to end like this. His mind was a raging cyclone of doubts. Everything that he had believed and trusted in for almost four years was slipping from his grasp. He thought that Jesus was the long awaited Messiah, the king of the Jews, the deliverer of the nation of Israel from the oppression of Rome, the establisher of the long lost throne of David. He looked at Him, arms tied behind Him, like an animal tethered to a post. He did not look much like a deliverer now. He looked like a man with no hope, like someone already resigned to His fate. He was obviously going to die and now, in this alien world of hostile religion, Peter's own life was in considerable danger. He thought of leaving. He was obviously a failure and a serious disappointment to Jesus. Yet one thing he was certain about, this Man was his best friend, and right now He needed some support, so there was no way that he could just walk away and leave Him. He had so many regrets. He wished that he had not fallen asleep in the garden. He wished he had not resorted to the sword when the mob came. If he had prayed and been more watchful, perhaps he could have warned Jesus about the approaching police and He would never have been arrested. He felt so guilty.

It was a long and arduous night as Jesus was interrogated, first by Annas and then by Caiaphas. Witness after witness was introduced to pronounce appalling lies and falsehoods against the Christ, but, to the frustration of His accusers, none were able to give them the excuse they were looking for to put Him to death. There were moments when Peter wanted to leap up and shout out in his friend's defence, but an uncharacteristic caution, bred in the womb of cowardice, prevailed to keep him silent. He was afraid and his fear conspired to justify the many doubts that were invading his troubled mind.

The girl who originally admitted him went off duty and her replacement was an alert young woman who was ambitious to please her employers. She carefully scrutinised the people present in the chamber at such an early hour and her eye fell upon Peter. He was still sitting by the fire, looking very much uncomfortable and out of place. She was suspicious. Perhaps he was some homeless vagrant, who had somehow managed to gain access to the building to shelter from the coldness of the night. She approached him slowly, circling to obtain a closer look at his face. An unsuspecting Peter obligingly raised his head and their eyes met. He quickly, too quickly, averted his eyes and turned his face back towards the non-threatening flames of the fire, but it was too late. All heads turned towards him as the girl challenged him.

"This man was also with Him," she alleged.

Peter was caught off guard and floundered in his embarrassment. His mind had been occupied with negatives and his thoughts and emotions were dominated by doubt. There was no time to analyse his position or carefully formulate a reply. His heart was exposed. Out of a doubting, cowardly heart, his mouth spoke his passionate denial.

"Woman, I know Him not!"

His face was flushed with the heat of panic and his throat constricted with the passage of his shameful words. As the denial left his lips, somewhere out in the darkness of Jerusalem, not too far away, a cock crew, somewhat prematurely, for it was still some time before dawn. His eyes darted across to where Jesus sat before His persecutors. He hoped that He had not heard. He didn't look as though He had. He was really frightened now, but breathed a slow sigh of relief as the unwelcome attention was lost in the distractions of the occasion. He waited for a few minutes before slowly standing and withdrawing quietly into the vestibule behind him. He was only a few steps from the street and safety, but still he could not bring himself to leave. He was trapped between cowardice and loyalty, afraid of the conflict which he could recognise within himself, yet unable to come to a decision one way or the other. He would never have thought of himself as a coward, but he could not deny the evidence of his actions and words. He stood, trembling slightly, nervously looking through the archway and across the courtyard to where Jesus was still standing.

"This fellow was also with Jesus of Nazareth."

The words were those of another house servant and were pronounced in a terrifyingly loud voice. The fact is that Peter was just too well known to hide his relationship with Jesus. He was one of His closest companions of four years standing and the most prominent of all the disciples. This second exposure of his alliance with Jesus produced a breathtaking panic in the fisherman and the blood pounded in his temples. His eyes flashed around the porch to assess the damage, whilst with his mouth he spontaneously denied the truth, this time with an oath.

"I do not know the man," he snapped.

Almost miraculously the people around him seemed to accept his protestation and within a few minutes he found himself alone in the spacious porch. The door to freedom beckoned invitingly and he seriously considered running out into the cold air of the early morning. Anywhere would do, just away from his fear, perhaps back to Galilee, back to the lake he loved, to the place where he was in control of his surroundings and his destiny. But still he could not leave, because, however fearful he was, however cowardly, he found it impossible to just walk away. He stood where he was, vacant, like a zombie, unable to make a positive decision one way or the other. Eventually his mind went to Jesus and he wondered what they were doing with Him now. He tentatively moved to the arch and looked across.

The Lord's persecutors had eventually produced two witnesses who claimed to have heard Jesus say that if the temple was destroyed, He was able to build it again in three days. Jesus refused to answer the accusation. Caiaphas rose to his feet. He was becoming frustrated and agitated with the proceedings, which seemed to be going nowhere.

"Answerest thou nothing? What is it that these witness against thee?"

Again with the calm dignity of a king, Jesus offered no reply. His eyes searched the face of the arrogant priest, unperturbed by his anger and not at all intimidated by his authority as chairman of the Sanhedrin. The Lord's refusal to answer inflamed Caiaphas and, burning with rage, he strode across and thrust his face only inches from that of the Saviour of the world. With undisciplined and unrestrained fury, he screamed at his prisoner in the name of the Almighty.

"I adjure thee by the living God, that thou tell us whether thou be the Christ, the Son of God."

His words were designed to extract an answer which would give the priests the damning evidence that they needed, to condemn Him for blasphemy. They also offered Jesus the opportunity to make a statement which would place Him in His Father's will, to drink the cup He had been offered in the garden and embrace the cross which would bring salvation to the world. This time He made a clear and unequivocal reply.

"I am," He said. "Hereafter shall ye see the Son of man sitting on the right hand of power, and coming in the clouds of heaven."

Caiaphas stood back and grasped the neck of his robe with two hands. With a dramatic gesture of triumphalism he ripped it down the middle. It was over! The Nazarene had spoken blasphemy! He immediately demanded judgement from his cohorts and, without hesitation, they pronounced Him worthy of death. There followed a most disgraceful display of violence and mockery. These so called holy men of religion began spitting in the face of Jesus, whilst beating Him with their fists. They then blindfolded Him and took it in turns to punch Him in the face, demanding that He use His prophetic talents to indentify His individual abusers.

Peter stood and watched the disgusting spectacle from the porch, where he had now stood for over an hour. No-one else had accosted him, or added to his fear. He was cold and tired and miserable. He moved back into the courtyard and once more approached the fire. He could see Jesus more clearly now. His persecutors removed the blindfold to reveal the bruised and bloodied face of his friend. Jesus turned and looked in Peter's direction. He watched through swollen eyes as his erring disciple warmed himself at the fire. How He loved this fisherman from Galilee, but how sad and disappointed He felt at his lack of strength and courage. He desperately wanted him to be Peter, not Simon. Where was "the rock"? It was crushed and sifted like wheat!

"Of a truth this fellow also was with Him: for he is a Galilean."

This time the words came from behind Peter, piercing his craven heart like an arrow of fire and triggering a surge of adrenaline which thumped like a hammer through his body and set his bloodstream racing with fear. He turned wide-eyed to face his accuser and found a whole group of people staring at him with scornful hostility. His belly turned over and his heart sank in him like a stone. The man who had spoken, now went on, "Surely thou also art one of them; for thy speech betrayeth thee."

Peter's knees felt weak and a wave of nausea rose from his stomach and, as it reached his brain, the room moved. His eyes were wild, like those of a trapped animal, and self preservation became his master. He began to swear and curse as he yielded fully to the demonic plan to bring him down. He screamed his denial with unrestrained abandonment.

"Man, I know not what thou sayest, I know not the man."

Then it happened. As the words echoed around the stunned chamber, at that precise moment, the cock crew for the second time and Peter remembered the warning that Jesus had given him only hours before, that, before the cock crew twice, he would deny Him three times. The sound of the cockerel crashed into his ears like a death sentence. It echoed and re-echoed in his mind, amplified a thousand times. The crowing took on the sound of hideous laughter, as though myriads of demons rejoiced at his demise. It seemed to Peter that the skies above Jerusalem were rocking with uncontrollable mirth and that, somewhere in the great beyond, the prince of darkness himself smugly smiled in celebration of his victory. He turned towards Jesus, desperately hoping that He had not seen or heard his sad betrayal, but He was already looking at him. The look said everything. It was a knowing look, but unutterably sad. It was even an understanding look, and the most powerful thing about it was that it was void of condemnation. Peter was a failure and a coward, and he knew it. At that moment he despised himself more than at any other time in his life. Without a second's hesitation and without a backward glance, he walked across the courtyard, through the ornate archway, out through the main door and into the street. There he stood for a minute, blinded by the tears of remorse which were already flooding his tired eyes.

Dawn was already breaking over the historic city of Jerusalem and the air was cold. At first he just ran. He ran down the cobbled streets until he put a safe distance between himself and the house of Caiaphas, then, hiding himself in a convenient doorway, he allowed the fountain of his emotions to break. He wept bitterly. Huge sobs, like boulders, rose from his belly and choked him with anguish. From his lips of denial came a painful wail of misery. His knees gave way beneath the weight of guilt and he slumped, broken and hopeless, into a heap of trembling flesh. His mind went back to a wonderful morning long ago in Capernaum when, on the deck of his boat, after the Lord had used the ship as a pulpit and then provided a miraculous catch of fish, he knelt before Jesus, saying, "Depart from me; for I am a sinful man, O Lord." They were words of humble surrender, spoken to express his feelings of unworthiness at being in the presence of One so holy. On that day the words were not intended to be taken literally, but now, by his actions and wicked denial of his Lord, he had dismissed Him from his life. He had walked away from the One for whom he had left everything. He had deserted the One he loved above all others. What a fool he was! He was engulfed with the emptiness of unalterable loss. He had no idea where to go, or what to do. Jesus once asked His disciples, "Will ye also go away?" It was Peter who answered with the question, "Lord, to whom shall we go? Thou hast the words of eternal life." Now he had "gone away", but there was nowhere to go. For the first time in his life he experienced the stark reality of naked loneliness. He wanted to go back and tell Jesus how sorry he was, but how could he do that? How hollow and meaningless it would sound. Anyway, he knew that he did not have the courage. He hated himself for what he had done, but he also knew that, given the same circumstances, he would do it again. He was still afraid, too afraid to go back. He stumbled like a drunken man from street to street. He met Mary the mother of Jesus, accompanied by the young man Mark, on her way to the house of Caiaphas. He blurted out his confession and hung his head in shame as she rushed on to find her Son.

He returned to Gethsemane and found some scant shelter under an olive tree. It felt strangely silent in the garden, the scene of a battle fought in the spiritual realm, won by Jesus, lost by Peter. He did not really understand why he had come here, perhaps to torment himself with guilt in the place where his betrayal of Christ had begun. Whatever, he fell into a fitful sleep and did not wake until the sun warmed him through the branches of the bush. His mind was immediately beset with the memories of the night and he wondered what had become of Jesus. The confusion and the doubt were still there. He did not understand the events taking place around him, but his overwhelming preoccupation was with his own failure. He found a place to wash himself and drank some water from the stream before heading out across the Kidron valley and slowly approaching the palace of Caiaphas. Everything was silent in the street outside the house and the doors were firmly closed. It was mid-morning and Peter found it difficult to imagine that Jesus was still being held there. He waited for an hour or more before the door opened and a servant girl skipped lightly into the street. Peter stepped forward and politely asked for news of the Nazarene who was tried in the judgement hall during the night. Was He still in the building and, if not, where had He been taken?

"He is not here sir," she replied. "He was taken from here in the night to answer before Pontius Pilate. I heard that He was sentenced to death by crucifixion. He could be dead by now, but I don't know."

It is a strange thing that a man who is afraid to die can want to die, but that is where Peter found himself. He was a coward in the face of death when he considered it his enemy, but from the moment he heard the news about Jesus, death became a possible friend. He could not bear to live with the guilt of what he had done. Like a man in a trance he walked the streets of the city, his mind flooded with memories and regrets. He found himself irresistibly drawn to the place outside the city wall, where the Romans performed their executions. Perhaps He wasn't dead! Perhaps He had performed one of His amazing miracles and disappeared from the midst of His enemies. It was approaching mid-day as he approached the fish gate to head out of the city. Suddenly the unusually hot spring day inexplicably cooled and a clammy mist settled over Jerusalem. He instinctively looked up and watched as heavy, dark clouds rolled across the heavens. The shroud of gloom thickened before his eyes until all light was extinguished and it became as dark as midnight. The city came to a stand-still before this strange phenomenon. People hurried from their pursuits to the safety of their homes and Roman soldiers returned to their barracks. Peter knew that this was no ordinary darkness. It was supernatural. He also knew that it had something to do with the arrest of Jesus. It was as though heaven itself was hiding some great shame from its view. He was afraid. He fell to his knees by the city gate and pressed his forehead into the dust.

"Oh God, forgive me for my sin. I am so sorry for denying your Son. I have betrayed Him in His hour of need and failed Him in His great trouble. He warned me and I did not give heed to His words. I fell a prey to my enemies and there is no way back. Have mercy on me Oh God, have mercy on me."

He remained on his knees in the darkness for a long time, until he eventually decided to head back into Jerusalem, to his friend John's house. Perhaps there he would obtain news about Jesus and at least be able to talk to some of the others. It was 3pm as he arrived at the house, only to find it locked up and empty. He walked round to the back of the house, pulled his cloak around him against the chill of the mist, and prepared to wait. As he did so the ground beneath him began to tremble, as Jerusalem quaked in the face of supernatural power. On a hill outside the city, the Son of God had cried, "It is finished!" and earth and hell trembled as heaven rejoiced. Peter was terrified! The earthquake rumbled on for about a minute and as the ground grew still the darkness lightened. The curtain of clouds unfolded and the mist dispersed before a gentle breeze. Within a few minutes the sun was shining from a cloudless sky.

It was about 7pm when John arrived home, supporting a weary looking Mary on his arm. John was the first to speak. He looked at his friend with eyes of compassion.

"Come inside Peter and have something to eat."

Peter broke into body wrenching sobs. It was obvious from Mary's demeanour that her Son was dead. John trimmed the candles and the three of them sat in the flickering light and talked of the happenings of the day. Peter wanted to know, but at the same time, was afraid to know. They told him about the horrors of Golgotha, the shame and the pain, and the words He had spoken from the cross. Peter wanted to know if He had mentioned him, but he was afraid to ask. He wondered if when Jesus prayed, "Father, forgive them, for they know not what they do", he could somehow be included. He doubted it, because he certainly did know what he was doing. He heard how Jesus cried out "My God, My God, why hast Thou forsaken Me?" He did not understand what that meant, but he knew that he had forsaken Jesus and it went like an arrow into his soul, as if He was crying, "Peter, Peter, why hast thou forsaken Me?" They told him how Jesus shouted "It is finished" just before the earthquake, and how the soldier thrust the spear into His side. Finally he was told how Joseph of Arimathea and Nicodemus had taken the body of Jesus, anointed it and wrapped it in linen and laid it in a borrowed tomb in the garden beneath Golgotha.

Jesus was dead. His best friend, his Lord, the Messiah, was dead, and the last words that He heard from Peter were words of denial, accompanied with oaths and cursing. He had failed Him at the last and there was now no possibility of ever making amends. He felt like a rat being shaken in the teeth of Satan. His enemy had him on the rack. A few more turns of the screw and he would be finished forever.

CHAPTER SEVEN

"Futures funeral I attend;
The past has no attraction;
Where can I go, when hope is vain,
And only memories remain?"

THE THREE DAYS FOLLOWING THE crucifixion of the Lord Jesus were a time of indescribable agony. Peter was not the kind of person to quickly disregard his failure and it would be a long time before he could even begin to forgive himself. Add to this, however, the activity of the demonic against his mental condition, and his mind was an agitated pool of guilt-oriented torment, from which there was no escape. Words of comfort and consolation from his friends were of little consequence and served only to add irritation to his relationships. He did not believe that he deserved their kindness and therefore rejected it with considerable annoyance. As far as he was concerned he had forfeited everything which he held dear and was unworthy of any opportunity to make amends. He was a man bereft of hope and he quickly descended into a pit of despair and self recrimination. His short periods of restless sleep were punctuated with nightmares of hideous crowing cockerels shrieking with demonic laughter as he slid a knife into the heart of Jesus. His nights were hell and his days were long hours of mental torment and spiritual sorrow. He was haunted with that last look of sadness and disappointment which he had seen in the eyes of Jesus, in the house of Caiaphas. A thousand "if only's" raced through his head. He repeatedly asked John to recount the details of the Lord's words from the cross, vainly hoping that perhaps his friend would suddenly remember something that Jesus had said about him, which would provide a modicum of comfort, but there was nothing to bring him peace. Even though he remained with the rest of the group, for fear of the Jews, he felt utterly alone. The others passed the time in debating, reminiscing, pondering, on past, present and future, but he had no part with it. He had destroyed all his tomorrows. For him the future did not exist. He had no real purpose in living anymore. His vision to become a "fisher of men" had been the central vision of his life and filled him with a passion which he could never feel for any other purpose. To serve Christ had been his only desire and could not now be replaced by the mundane. He had foolishly thrown away the gold, but he certainly was not prepared to settle for the dross. He knew that to taste the divine presence, experience the love of God, grasp the spiritual vision and commit to the building of the kingdom of heaven, was an irreplaceable ambition which had spoiled him for everything else. He was lost! Finished! It would have been better had he never met Jesus that day at Bethabara, or heard Him say, "Thou art Peter, and upon this rock I will build my church". Some rock he was! A rock of offence to the very One he had pledged to follow! A thousand times he whispered "I am so sorry" to the wind and his tears of remorse seemed to know no end. But he could find no balm for his tortured soul and only the darkness of eternal loss lay before him.

Early in the morning of the first day of the week, three days after the death of Jesus, Peter was awakened from a fragile sleep by another trembling of the earth. It was, if anything, more violent than the earthquake which shook Jerusalem on the day of the crucifixion. It lasted for about one minute, but it amplified his vulnerability. He felt as though the eternal God was indignantly searching for the one who had transgressed His purposes. He lay still for a while, until it appeared that the danger had passed, before joining the others in the main area of the house. They were expressing considerable concern for Mary, the mother of Jesus, her sister Salome, and Mary Magdalene, who had left some time before dawn to go to the tomb and anoint the body of Jesus. They must have been caught up in the quake and some of the group wanted to go and find them. Others, however, were more sensitive to the women's desire to be alone at the tomb and did not wish to infringe upon their privacy. Peter felt that he had no right to offer an opinion about anything and remained silent. They did not, however, have long to wait. The sun had barely warmed the streets of Jerusalem, when the three women exploded onto the scene. The feeling in the house was not good. Peter was a powerful personality, with a huge presence, and his gloom and depression tended to overpower the atmosphere. It was, however, no match for the excitement and joy which accompanied the women as they rushed in. They were buzzing with life, all trying to talk at the same time, and radiating such happiness, that the misery of the last days was expelled with the speed at which light expels darkness. They were chattering about Jesus being alive, telling a preposterous story of an empty tomb and angels in white raiment. They told how, when they arrived at the garden, the stone was already rolled away from the tomb and how the angel had asked them, "Why seek ye the living amongst the dead?" It frankly, all sounded rather absurd and most of the people in the room were unashamedly sceptical. They considered the women to be in an unstable emotional condition and refused to believe that their story was anything more than wishful thinking, a figment of their imagination, or that they were possibly the victims of some cruel contrivance of the Roman guards. Mary Magdalene looked earnestly into the face of Peter.

"Listen Peter! We took oil and spices, with which to anoint the body of the Lord. On our way to the tomb there was an earthquake. You must have felt the earthquake?" She paused and waited for Peter to confirm. He did so with a nod of his head. "When the danger was over we carried on and entered the garden, but when we reached the tomb the stone which sealed the mouth of the sepulchre was already rolled back from the entrance. We were afraid, but we slowly approached the tomb and went inside." Her eyes flooded with tears and she gripped her friend's arm. "Peter, it was empty! The body was not there! But sitting in the place where the body of Jesus had lain was the most amazing man I have ever seen. He was clothed in brilliant white garments and his face was like the face of an angel. He stood up to greet us and, as he did so, another, of the same kind, appeared with him. The first one spoke to us and said, 'Ye seek Jesus of Nazareth, which was crucified: He is risen; He is not here: behold the place where they laid Him. But go your way, tell His disciples and Peter that He goeth before you into Galilee.' We turned and ran like the wind. We have run all the way home. Peter, Jesus is alive and the angel specifically said that we should tell you. Go Peter, go and see for yourself."

Simon Peter looked calmly into the face of his friend, Mary, and he knew that she was speaking the truth. His heart was racing and an explosive mixture of emotions was surging through his body. He did not reply and his eyes never left hers as he fastened his tunic. Then he turned on his heel and, without a word to the others, left the house, closely followed by John, the son of Zebedee. The two of them ran through the streets of Jerusalem, oblivious to the puzzled expressions of the people of the city, who were now going about their daily business. Out through the city gate they went, and on towards the hill called Golgotha and the garden which nestled at its base. John outran his older friend and arrived before him, but stopped reverently at the mouth of the open tomb, pensively looking in, as though afraid of what he might find within. Peter, breathless but determined, arrived and without hesitation, stepped inside. The two of them stood together in the half light and stared at the place where the body of their Lord was supposed to be. The linen shroud was there, neatly folded, and the soudarion, which was the separate material used for the binding of the head, folded and placed apart from the main shroud. The amazing thing was that the material had not been unwound. The body had somehow disappeared from within the grave clothes without disturbing them. Peter wiped his eyes with his sleeve. Tears of wonderment flowed down the faces of both men. How holy was this sacred place.

The friends emerged from the tomb, excited, but controlled. They believed! There was no doubt! By some amazing miracle, Jesus had been raised from the dead! The women's story was true!

Mary Magdalene followed Peter and John back to the garden and they found her standing excitedly, eagerly waiting for their response. The unbelief of the others had fed thoughts of doubt into her mind. Was it possible that someone could have stolen His body? If so, she wanted to know where he had been taken. Peter spent a few minutes speaking with Mary, while John thoughtfully headed back home. He sought to encourage her as best he could, but he was facing new battles of his own. He finally left her, weeping and confused, in the seclusion of the garden and made his way back towards the city. A few minutes later, Mary became the first person to actually speak with the risen Christ, at first mistaking Him for the gardener.

Peter had a lot to think about. He believed that Jesus was alive, but he did not know how to deal with this new turn of events. Once again, his mind was a morass of disjointed thoughts. Why had the angel said to the women, "Tell His disciples and Peter?" Perhaps he was not regarded as a disciple anymore? Perhaps they were words designed to remind him of his failure, words of condemnation? Or could it be that they conveyed a message of forgiveness? Perhaps Jesus was saying, "Tell Peter, let him know that, despite everything, I still care." Or perhaps it wasn't true at all. Perhaps the Romans had taken the body somehow, and the women in their emotional confusion had imagined the visitation of the angels. He did not really believe that. In his heart he knew that it was true. Jesus was alive, but he was not sure that he wanted to see Him. He was too ashamed to look Him in the face.

Deep in contemplation he passed through the Fish Gate and on into the city, wending his way through the narrow back-streets towards John's house. He turned a corner as he approached the vicinity of home and opened his mouth to give the days greetings to a man that was walking towards him. The salutation froze on his lips. There He was! Jesus! Just a few paces away! He was alive! Peter came to an immediate halt and for a moment their eyes met. It was only for one, brief moment, but it seemed an eternity. Silent communication flowed between the two men, before Peter lowered his eyes in agonising shame and nervously straightened the girdle about his waist. He slowly raised his head once more, but He was gone. He ran back to the corner, but Jesus was nowhere to be seen. He ran in the direction of his travel, but He was not there either. It was as though some unseen hand had spirited him away. Not a word had passed between them, but there was no doubt that he had seen the Lord. He ran the rest of the way home.

It was later that evening, having already appeared to two of the disciples on the road to Emmaus, that Jesus visited the whole group, that is, with the exception of Thomas, who was not present. He appeared so unexpectedly, in the middle of the room, that they were all terrified, thinking that they were seeing a ghost, but He showed them the nail prints in His hands and feet and invited them to hold Him and touch Him. This was no spirit. He was alive and physical. He asked for food and they brought Him broiled fish and a honeycomb, and He ate before them. They were all ecstatic with joy, all, that is, except Peter. He felt uncomfortable and ashamed. He stood behind the others as they crowded around Jesus, avoiding making eye contact with the man he had denied. Guilt and shame formed a mountainous barrier between him and his Lord. He wanted to say "sorry", but he knew how empty it would sound, how utterly disproportionate to his crime. Part of him wanted Jesus to speak to him, even if only to rebuke him for his cowardice. At least that would break the ice. But He said nothing. It seemed that Jesus had no interest in speaking a word to His friend. He never even looked in his direction, or acknowledged that he was in the room. The atmosphere between them was tense and Peter was relieved when Jesus finally departed. The others were chattering with excitement, seemingly oblivious to Peter's pain, so he again slipped out into the night and once more gave way to tears of heart-wrenching remorse.

He continued to live in his own private hell of sorrow for another week before Jesus appeared once more to His disciples. Again, no words passed between Jesus and Peter. The Lord took no initiative to communicate with him and Peter was too embarrassed to venture an apology, or to make an attempt at reconciliation. He felt more hopeless than ever, because he interpreted the Lord's silence as a personal rejection. Not that he blamed Him. He deserved to be rejected.

It was in many ways a peculiar situation for them all. They were obviously thrilled and excited that Jesus was alive, but perplexed that He was no longer with them. Their whole manner of life was now different. Before His crucifixion Jesus lived with them. They worked with Him every day. Now, they had no idea where He was, what He was doing, or where He lived. He had only visited them twice and they had no idea when He would appear again. They did not know what to do, or where to go. One thing was certain; they could not just live a life of seclusion, waiting for Him to show Himself. They needed to earn some money and find some kind of security for their lives. The days of travelling everyday with Jesus, listening to Him teach and preach, were obviously over. They felt very much alone in a hostile world.

Peter's mind instinctively turned to his beloved Galilee. Perhaps they should return to Capernaum. At least there they would feel free to move about, without fear of arrest or persecution. Then he remembered. Had not the angels in the tomb instructed the women to tell His disciples that He was going before them into Galilee? Perhaps that is what they should all do; leave Jerusalem and return to Galilee. He felt better already, at the thought of Capernaum, the lake, his own house, and his much loved Joanna. Perhaps he could put the agony of the last few weeks out of his mind and begin to build some kind of future.

So the confused and emotionally ragged group of disciples, headed north, away from the city and its politics and religious hypocrisy, to the natural beauty and tranquillity of Galilee. The familiar sights and scenery were pleasing to Peter, but his pleasure was alloyed with the memories of the last three years of working with Jesus. This was not only the scene of Peter's upbringing and youth, but the setting for the majority of Jesus' ministry. His emotional response to familiar places was mixed and by no means as easy to deal with as he anticipated. He found that he did not relate to Capernaum as the exciting place he knew as a child and later as a fisherman, but as the place where he served Jesus. His memories were not of that which he had given up, but of that which he had lost. Capernaum felt like a place where someone had died. Jesus was not there to meet them. He was conspicuous by His absence. The place at the edge of the lake where Jesus first called them to follow Him, the site of His preaching from Peter's boat, the Synagogue where Jesus healed the demoniac, even his own house which the Master had adopted as His home and the place where He healed Joanna's mother, were all reminders of something lost. Capernaum without Jesus was like an empty shell and exposed a massive vacuum in Peter's soul. Instead of escaping his guilt, the move from Jerusalem seemed to increase it. His remorse raged like a fire in his heart and pulled him down into a deepening depression. He stood and gazed across the surface of Lake Galilee. Thomas was with him and James and John, and three of the others. His life was being swallowed by his failure.

"I'm going fishing," he said.

His voice was hollow, aimless, lost and hopeless. He wasn't asking anybody to go with him. He did not even consider the fact that he no longer had a boat. He just said it, because that is what he wanted to do. His dull, empty eyes were lost in the gentle rise and fall of the water. He was guided by the guilt of failure, his inability to cope with the change which was so obviously upon them, and the necessity to make money, now that their ministry had ceased.

Surprisingly, his six colleagues were instantly ready to go with him. Peter almost expected them to lecture him for suggesting a return to that which he had left behind. He knew that it was a negative step and braced himself for an argument with his friends, but no protest came. They were motivated by the need for finance and were ready to join him as he returned to his natural comfort zone. Peter used his considerable influence to hire the necessary boat and equipment and, for the first time in nearly four years, he and his friends pushed out onto the lake. Perhaps the wind and the spray and the smell of the sea and the fish would blow away the torment and the shame from his heart and grant him the elusive peace his soul craved. He laughed as he swung the boat to catch the breeze and happily shouted instructions to his fellow fishermen, but it was all a facade. His heart was not in it and an awful void expanded in his soul as he vainly tried to recapture the thrill of a past life. He knew that he was not supposed to be there! It simply was not the same! There was no atmosphere, no purpose, and no life! Only the memory of the words of the Christ echoing in his conscience, rising above the noises of the sea,

"Follow Me, and I will make you fishers of men."

Chapter Eight

"From darkest night emerges dawn;
From sorrows womb, new hope is born;
When all seems lost, and trust is slain,
He stands to be my friend again"

Darkness fell across Lake Galilee, otherwise called the Sea of Tiberias, after the capital city of Galilee, which graced its western bank, but the waters were calm and a full moon cast its orange glow across its gently moving floor. On any other occasion, under any other circumstances, the men would have enjoyed the sheer beauty of the night, the light reflecting from the surface of the water, and the dark silhouette of the mountains to the east, framing the scene against a clear night sky. A myriad stars glittered like a canopy of tiny lights above them and the only sound was the lapping of the water against the creaking timbers of the ship. They worked as hard as they had ever worked and applied every skill they had learned from childhood, but they caught no fish. Their voices carried across the placid surface of the lake as they called instructions, made suggestions and cast their nets, but it was all in vain. The fish were nowhere to be found. For Peter it was the final insult to his pride. He knew that he had failed Jesus. He had proved himself a complete failure in his calling to be a fisher of men, but now he could not even do what he had done since he was a small boy. He could not even catch fish.

Time progressed to the fourth watch of the night and he remembered how on a former night, one of more stormy proportions, at 3am, Jesus had come to their rescue, walking on the water. His eyes involuntarily scanned the surface of the lake. No Jesus would come walking to his aid tonight. He felt empty inside. He felt sick with nostalgic sorrow. What a change had taken place since that amazing night, when faith rose up in his heart and he strode, hand in hand with Jesus, across the billowing waves. Now he had no faith. He had thrown it away to save his own miserable life. Never again would he experience the incredible friendship with the Son of God that he had engaged that night, a friendship which defied natural laws and produced the impossible. He had betrayed it to his everlasting sorrow. He sat defeated in the stern of the boat and in a subdued and disconsolate voice, addressed his companions.

"I am so sorry my friends, but we should never have come out here tonight. It was a mistake. My whole life is just one long mistake. I do not know what to do, or where to go."

"We must trust Peter. The Lord has not brought us this far to forsake us now. It is just a little confusing at the moment, but we should remember that Jesus has been raised from the dead. This is just the beginning. All is not lost. We must have faith."

"Not me John! I have no faith! I can no longer trust, because I betrayed the trust He placed in me. I failed him John, and I fear that, for me, there is no way back."

The first hint of dawn was paling the sky beyond the mountains, as the disciples turned the bow of their boat towards the shore, to head for home. They had caught nothing and, since the brief exchange of words between Peter and John, no-one had spoken. There was nothing much to say. The only sound was the screech of an occasional gull, out too soon to welcome the coming morn. The lone figure of a man was standing watching them from the shore, not an unusual occurrence at the break of day, as early risers enjoyed a walk by the water, savouring the quiet beauty of the lake before breakfast. It was a peaceful scene, but Peter was a broken man, weeping in inconsolable grief in the hinder part of the ship. He had never felt as low as this. He wanted to die.

"Hey, lads, have you caught any fish?"

It was the stranger, calling to them from the beach. There was a short pause before Nathanael, rather grumpily, called back in the negative. The rest of them ignored the intrusion and urged the boat in the direction of the landing place. The man on the beach shouted to them again,

"If you cast your net on the right side of the ship, you will catch fish."

Nathanael laughed and Thomas muttered a disrespectful comment under his breath. The man was mad. Who did he think he was? The suggestion was absurd. If they had caught no fish throughout the entire night and there were no fish on the left side of the boat, how could there possibly be fish on the right side, and how could a man who had probably never done a day's fishing in his life, possibly know? It was a suggestion which needed to be treated with polite contempt.

John, however, was standing at the side of the boat, hand raised as a visor above his eyes, gazing intently through the light early morning mist which was rolling gently across the still water, at the man who was standing on the shore. There was something familiar about him, something recognisable about the man's voice, something compelling about his command. John spoke quietly, but it was an order, not a request.

"Just do it!" he said. "Just do it!"

Peter watched, disconsolately, as his friends obediently pooled their efforts and dropped the nets over the right hand side of the ship. Instantly he felt the boat list crazily and the starboard lip of the craft dipped dangerously close to the water. They began to heave and pull at the laden net in an attempt to secure the catch, but all their efforts to bring the nets on board were in vain. It became obvious that the only way to land the fish was to bring the boat to the beach with the heavy net still submerged, no small task to accomplish, but adrenaline flowed and reserves of energy were plentiful. John gripped Peter's arm and voiced the thoughts of every man on board.

"Peter! It is the Lord!"

A surge of excitement, mingled with a terrible apprehension, ran through Peter's burly frame. He was instantly torn between two emotions. A part of him wanted to see Jesus, but another part of him felt that he could not cope with another rebuff. He was too ashamed to take the initiative himself and venture an apology to Jesus, but another potential uncomfortable silence between them was too much to contemplate. He was convinced that Jesus had no place for him in His future plans. He probably wanted nothing more to do with him at all, for any purpose. He did sometimes incubate some resentment that Jesus was prepared to talk to all the others, but not to him. With the exception of John, they had all forsaken Him that night in the garden, but at least he had followed Him to the judgement hall. The others did not even have the courage to do that. His torment and confusion deepened by the day and Jesus suddenly showing up like this did not help his emotional state. He stood to his feet. He was naked, as were they all. It was easier to fish without the encumbrance of wet clothes, especially when the nights were reasonably warm. They wore their fishers coats until they were out on the lake, discarded them for work and put them on again as they approached the shore. He gazed across the slowly narrowing divide at the figure of the man he had wronged and the voice of satanic hatred shouted in his head.

"Die, Peter! End it! You are finished! Take a look at Him! You forsook Him! There is no way back! Do you think He will ever forget what you did to Him? Stop fighting it! You cannot go on like this! Let the water that you walked on be your grave!"

Peter listened to the voices in his head and he agreed. He needed to accept that his life was now useful to no-one. He donned his coat to hide his nakedness and, giving no-one time to protest, leaped into the sea. He allowed himself to sink below the surface of the cold water, but instinctively began to swim. He wanted to die, but was too afraid to allow death to take him. His heavy coat hindered his ability to swim, dragging him under, but he fought his way to the surface and filled his lungs with the morning air. The voices of his demon enemies were screaming in his mind.

"Die Peter! Give it up! If you reach the shore He will reject you! You denied Him! It's over."

He tried to swim towards the shore. He could hear his friends shouting to him, urging him to return to the boat, but he ignored their pleas. He was double-minded. He knew that if he gave in, it would all be over in a few minutes. Then he thought of his beautiful Joanna. She had done nothing to deserve the sorrow and pain that his selfishness would bring upon her. But he felt so weary. The coat was so heavy, too heavy to contend with. Once again he slid beneath the waves and he could hear the demons laughing at his demise. Then he heard the words of Jesus, "Satan hath desired to have you Peter, that he may sift you as wheat, but I have prayed for you, that your faith fail not." He said "I have prayed for you!" He must care! He could feel consciousness slipping away from him, but the words "I have prayed for you" were a lifeline to his drowning soul. He pulled his arms from the coat, allowing it to drift into the cold dark depths, and struck for the surface. He sucked the life giving air into his bursting lungs, composed himself, relaxing to regain his strength, and then began swimming slowly towards the shore.

He lay naked and exhausted in the warmth of the early morning sunshine. He could see the Lord a little further up the beach tending a brightly burning fire. He could hear the cracking of the wood as it fell victim to the flames and he could smell the aroma of freshly cooking fish. He stayed exactly where he was, not feeling too good, and watched his comrades bring the boat to land. They disembarked and excitedly ran across to where Jesus was cooking breakfast. He told them to go and bring the fish that they had caught, but Peter strode across to the boat and its heaving net.

"I'll see to it," he called. He was in no hurry for his meeting with Jesus. He would rather work. So he single-handedly pulled the net ashore and counted one hundred and fifty three of the largest fish he had ever seen in Lake Galilee.

"Come and eat," Jesus called, and the hungry men gathered around the fire, drying their coats and warming their bellies with the food. Peter found a piece of sacking in the boat, tied it around his waist and nervously joined the men. He sat at the edge of the circle, deliberately out of eye contact with Jesus, but pleading inside for an end to the painful distance he felt between them. They finished eating, some of them lying back in blissful contentment, to soak up the rays of the strengthening sun. It was then that Jesus spoke, to Peter.

"Simon, son of Jonas, lovest thou me more than these?"

The words were designed to test Peter's true state of heart. Would he react defensively to being addressed as Simon instead of by the name that Jesus had given to him? Would the man who had so confidently predicted that, though everyone else might fail, he would never fail, even at the cost of prison or death, still claim to love Jesus more than his fellows? The question implied that Jesus believed that the others loved Him. Did Peter claim to love Him more than they did?

These were the first words that Jesus had spoken to Peter since He told him to put his sword away in Gethsemane and they went like a knife into his heart. He knew that he had failed. Of course he did not love Jesus more than the others. His actions had proved that. He could not even claim to love Him at all, not in the deepest meaning of the word. He loved Him as a dear friend, he was sure of that, but the days of idle words and fanciful claims were over.

"Lord, you know that I love you as my friend."

Gone is the bold, brash, over confident Peter of the past. He was basically saying, "Lord, I dare not claim to love you as I should, certainly not more than these others, but I do know that I love you, and you must know that too."

Jesus looked deep into the hurting soul of His servant and said, "Feed my lambs."

Peter was not sure what He meant by that, but it sounded like Jesus was somehow prepared to trust him with some kind of ministry, perhaps to young ones, or people newly converted. He was deeply touched with such gracious words. What kind of mercy was this that was prepared to trust one who had proven to be so unworthy of trust? He wanted to say more, to tell Him how he really felt, but a new humility now guarded his lips. He looked into the embers of the dying fire and remembered that it was when sitting warming himself at a fire that he had denied His Lord. The other six men were silent, respectful, each of them conscious of their own shortcomings.

"Simon, son of Jonas, lovest thou me?"

Jesus was repeating the question, but this time without comparing his love with that of the others. He was just presenting the challenge, irrespective of what anybody else thought or felt; did Peter love Him? Again Peter answered in the affirmative, but again he fell short of the claim to absolute love. He loved him as a friend. He was very fond of

Him. The Lord Jesus paused, prodding the fire with a stick, reminiscent of a former time when He had drawn in the sand whilst waiting for an answer from the woman taken in adultery. Then He said, "Shepherd my sheep." He went beyond instructing Peter to feed His lambs. He indicated that He wanted him to be responsible for caring for His entire flock. Peter remembered the past words of Jesus, when He said to him, "Upon this rock I will build my church." He felt a blend of hope and humility rising together in his heart, like the advent of a new dawn in his life.

Then there came the shocking third question. Three times Peter had denied his Lord and he knew that it was fitting that he should be challenged three times concerning his love. It was not the fact that it was the third challenge which upset Peter, but the fact that the Lord now appeared to question his sincerity in loving Him as a friend. This time He did not ask him, "Do you love me?" but, "Are you really fond of me? Do you love me as a friend?" Peter was afraid to claim to love Him as he once thought he had, but he was certain that he loved Him as a friend. To have this brought into question grieved him deeply and his reply contained passion, an enthusiasm and confidence which was unaffected by his failure.

"Lord, you know all things; you know that I love you as my friend."

The Master smiled. Of course He knew. He knows everything; but Peter needed the process. He needed to learn to measure his words and not to make spontaneous claims which were not true. The Lord knew that Peter was "very fond" of Him. He also knew that he loved Him, even with that highest form of love. The horror of recent days had done its work in His servant's life and Jesus knew that he would never deny Him again. Satan had asked to sift him to destruction, but, through the prayers of Jesus, that which was intended for evil was used to change this fisherman from boy to man. Peter had come of age. He was different, not that he was in a place where he would never make any more mistakes, but he had learned a huge and vital lesson. He was now ready to lead by example and strengthen his brothers, not with the flamboyant energy of the flesh, but with a heart humbled by failure and touched by divine mercy. The reply to his third and passionate response to his Lord's question came as before.

"Feed my sheep."

The commission was complete. He told him to feed the young, shepherd the mature, and then He told him to give spiritual food to the mature that they might grow more like their Saviour. Peter was indeed to be "Peter", a foundation rock in the universal church. Satan's hatred was used to discipline, refine, strengthen and prepare one of his greatest enemies for battle.

Jesus stood up to leave. His task for the morning was complete. Peter stood with Him, a bedraggled looking figure, naked but for the rags around his waist, but his eyes were shining with joyous relief. Jesus placed His hand upon the shoulder of His friend and reminded him that when he was young, he dressed himself and went where he chose to go, but advised him that, in his old age, he would be bound and taken where he would not choose to be taken. Peter looked into the eyes of his Lord and knew that He was being informed of a future day, when he would be asked to lay down his life for His Lord. He was being told that the very thing which he had so foolishly declared that he would do and then miserably failed in, he would accomplish in later life. He heard it, but he felt no fear, only an incredible sense of privilege, that the terrified coward who had stood that shameful night in the house of Caiaphas and denied with cursing that he had ever known Jesus, was being granted a second opportunity to be faithful.

They trudged through the sloping shingle, up to the path which led from the lake. The sun was warm on Peter's back, but the warmth and joy which filled his heart was beyond description. He felt so free! It was over! He was back! He turned and smiled at his friend John, who was just a few paces behind them. What a wonderful friend he was; reliable, faithful, strong and dependable.

"Lord, and what shall this man do?"

He motioned with his hand towards John. Jesus turned and faced Peter, placing his hands, one on each of his shoulders, with careful deliberation. He looked into his face. His eyes were scolding, but with a hint of amusement, like a father lifting a cautioning finger to a little boy.

"If it is my will, that he remain alive until I return again to the earth, what does that have to do with you Peter? You just concentrate on following me."

He swung on his heel and walked quickly up the path. Thomas was shouting from the boat.

"Eh! You two! What about all these fish?"

CHAPTER NINE

———

"He left! The heavens veiled His face;
To me bequeathed a universal task;
But how can I, unworthy, fill this post,
Unless He send me first, The Holy Ghost?"

F OR A TOTAL OF FORTY days Jesus visited His disciples after His resurrection, showing Himself to be alive by many infallible proofs. The relationship between Him and His followers was completely different from the pre-crucifixion period and they continued to be confused and perplexed about the future. Jesus was alive, but they were very much on their own, a fact which they found difficult to come to terms with. They discussed, at length, the strange conversation which took place in the upper room on the night of the betrayal of Jesus, a conversation which they obviously understood very little about at the time, but now seemed to be taking on more significance. He told them at that time, that He was going to leave them, but assured them that they would not be left alone. He was going to ask the Father to send to them the Holy Spirit, to walk with them and be in them. He said that He would direct them, teach them, lead them into all truth and would testify of Jesus Christ. He would come from the Father, as a part of the Godhead, and would be their constant companion, both individually and collectively. He would never leave them. Jesus also indicated that the Holy Spirit would have a universal impact. God with man would no longer be confined to a body, as Jesus had been, but be free to convict men and women of sin, righteousness and judgement, on a worldwide scale. Jesus actually said that it was expedient for Him to leave, because it was now essential, both for them and the world that the Holy Spirit should come.

In the sombre atmosphere that pervaded the upper room on that dark night of oppression and pending death, they had not particularly wanted to hear about a replacement for Jesus. They preferred to believe that He would not leave them and that He would become the king they believed He was born to be. Now, in these new circumstances, when Jesus was seldom with them, the idea of another comforter to be with them, and in them, was becoming a more attractive proposition.

When the forty days were expired and the time came for Jesus to finally take leave of His disciples and return home to the Father, He met with them one final time. They knew that this was the moment of goodbye and emotions were running high. There would be no more visits, no more encouraging conversations, no more guidance from the lips of wisdom. They would never sit and eat with Him again, not until that great day of reunion, when the whole of the ransomed throng will share in the Marriage Supper of the Lamb in the eternal world. Peter looked worried. He watched as Mary tearfully embraced her son for the last time. It was a moving scene. He realised as never before, the pain and suffering endured by this amazing woman in the cause of giving Christ to the world. He saw the tears of a son in the eyes of Jesus. His garments were blowing in the wind as He lifted his hands in blessing and the hair was blown back from His face, revealing the deep scars where the thorns had so cruelly pierced His brow. How He loved these men, whom He had called to carry the Gospel to the world! He urged them to wait in Jerusalem until the Holy Spirit arrived. They needed His power before they could do anything. Without Him they were useless. Jesus now referred to the coming of the Holy Spirit as a baptism, which reminded Peter of the baptism which John the Baptist practised at the Jordan. How could they be baptised in God? They could not possibly understand the mystery of such a thing, but they certainly got the message that the Holy Spirit was not going to arrive incognito. They were about to be saturated in God and His power, as surely as they were once soaked in the waters of the Jordan, but this time the drenching was to be internal as well as external. The Comforter was to come upon them and dwell within them and the effect would be to give them power, an internally generated power, which would enable them to be witnesses to Christ's reality, locally and also to the uttermost parts of the earth.

So He blessed them and embraced them and turned His eyes heavenward. Peter wanted to hold onto Him. Plentiful tears were flowing down his weather hardened face. He wanted to say sorry just once more, but the feet of His Saviour and Lord were slowly lifting from the earth, defying gravity, just as once they had mastered the stormy waters of the Galilee. Peter reached out and touched Him one final time, as He rose in veiled majesty from the mount. They all stood together, those friends of the Son of God, eyes and faces upward, as a cloud received Him out of their sight. They continued to gaze, hoping to catch another glimpse of Him through a gap in the clouds, but He was gone. His work was accomplished. An era had ended and a new one begun.

Heaven stood to welcome home its greatest Son and the hosts of heaven sang the victory song and gave everlasting glory to the Lamb.

Peter was the last to lower his gaze. Mary was weeping and John was offering her comfort. Eventually they all turned to head back down the slope to the city, occasionally looking up into the now cloudless sky. Two strangers stood before them, resplendent in their white apparel, perhaps the same two angels who had attended the empty tomb of Jesus six weeks before. One of them addressed the bewildered group, kindly, but firmly, seeking to bring their futile observations to an end, whilst also leaving on record a promise to God's people until the end of time.

"Ye men of Galilee, why stand ye gazing up into heaven? This same Jesus, who is taken up from you into heaven, shall so come in like manner as ye have seen Him go into heaven."

Peter smiled weakly, shrugging his ample shoulders in a gesture of resignation and turned away, leading his sad friends away from the scene. The angels departed. An uncommon chill wind was blowing across Olivet, adding to the lonely sense of desolation they were all experiencing. Despite the words of the angels, there was more than one glance back and up at the sky, as they made their way through the city and back to the upper room.

It was ten days before the Holy Spirit arrived; ten days of fellowship, prayer and waiting. The disciples had absolutely no idea what to expect, or how they would know when He had arrived. They knew that they would somehow have more power when He arrived, and Peter was more than aware that he needed that, in abundance. He was so thankful that he had recovered from the nightmare of his failure, but was now more conscious of his potential weaknesses than ever before. He was stripped of self confidence and alert to his need. Without the constant guidance and discipline which he had received from Jesus, he felt lost and vulnerable. He needed and wanted this promised Comforter from the Father and the accompanying power. If he was to fulfil the commission to preach the Gospel and make disciples of all nations, then he must have something far more than he presently possessed. Out of the one hundred and twenty followers of Jesus who crowded into the upper room, there was no-one more passionate in his waiting, than Simon Peter.

It was on the day of Pentecost, fifty days after the Passover that their new helper arrived. They had eaten breakfast and were united in a perfect blend of love, purpose and expectation. A wonderful sense of expectation filled the atmosphere, as they joined together in a time of prayer and worship. They poured out their hearts to the Almighty. Then a sudden hush fell upon them all. A silence which could be felt overwhelmed the group, no-one daring to speak. Far away, in the distance, they heard a sound like the rumbling of thunder, or that of an approaching mighty wind. It grew in intensity until it became a frightening roar. The building began to shake, as though in the grip of an earthquake, and then it was amongst them, swirling, powerful, supernatural, a wind issuing from the very essence of Divinity. This was the wind which had breathed across the waters at the beginning of time when God said, "Let there be light." This was the wind which blew down the valley of dry bones in the time of Ezekiel, until an army of resurrected soldiers stood upon their feet. This was God the Holy Ghost, come to baptise the church of Jesus Christ with a power they had never before known; the power to take the world.

Peter stood with rapt amazement, as what appeared to be flames of fire, appeared above the heads of the assembled people. The room was so full of God, the atmosphere so impregnated with the Divine power, that it seemed to him that he was receiving this Holy Comforter into the fountain of his spirit with every breath that he took, like he was being indwelt, his body becoming the temple of Almighty God Himself. He felt exhilarated by the purity of the Spirit. What an honour this was! What unparalleled mercy had taken him from the fishing boats of Capernaum, guided him through painful discipline and crippling failure, and brought him to this? He fell to his knees. He could feel the presence of the absent Christ. He began to weep as he realised that the Spirit of God had brought back to them the unseen Jesus; so that He who had been with them, might now be in them. His whole being was vibrating with power, not the transient flush of emotional reaction, but through the infilling of a pure and holy glory. He felt as though it was too much to contain, like he was about to explode. He just wanted to worship Him. He opened his mouth to offer his praise to God and from deep within there erupted an anthem of adoration, which left his lips in the words of a language which he had never learned. And it flowed like a river. Rivers of living water flowed from the belly of this unworthy man and his voice rose in triumphant exaltation of his Lord in languages which by-passed his intellect and understanding. He became aware that the same astonishing phenomenon was happening to everybody in the room. Upwards of one hundred and twenty people were magnifying God in languages other than their own. A great roar of adoration, a symphony of worship, an orchestration of inspired praise, rose into the heavens and out onto the surrounding streets of Jerusalem. The Holy Spirit had arrived and the apostles wait was over.

It is, of course, predictable, that news of such sensational happenings as these would spread quickly. It was barely nine o'clock in the morning, but the surrounding streets began to fill with inquisitive people, anxious to discover the source of the noise. Jerusalem was a cosmopolitan city, with numerous representatives from many different parts of the world. Although Jewish cynics were immediately dismissing the scenes emanating from the upper room as emotional insanity, or an exhibition of drunkenness, many of these foreigners were excitedly claiming that these unlearned followers of Jesus, were speaking in their native languages. There was genuine incredulity that these Galilean fishermen and others, were suddenly able to speak fluently in a diversity of languages. The streets around the centre of the sensation were buzzing with excitement, speculation and counter speculation. The arrival of the Holy Spirit had gathered a congregation together to hear about the Lord Jesus and Peter was about to make his debut as a public speaker empowered with the Holy Ghost.

Accompanied by the eleven apostles he rose to his feet and called the company to order. There was something remarkably different about him. He was calm, completely controlled, yet possessed of an authority which commanded respect. Gone was the coward of the judgement hall. The man, who previously had hidden away for fear of the Jews, now stood to challenge them directly. He was fearless and his words flowed without hesitation.

First he protested that he and his companions in the upper room were not drunk. He pointed out that such an accusation was in any circumstances ridiculous, as it was only 9am. They were, in fact, rather fortunate recipients of the fulfilment of a prophesy, uttered by the Jewish prophet, Joel, eight hundred years before. He proceeded to praise Jesus of Nazareth, reminding them of His miracles, and then accused them directly of complicity in His death. He spoke at some length concerning the indisputable evidence concerning His resurrection, announcing that Jesus was indeed the Messiah, and called his audience to repentance and baptism in the name of Jesus Christ, for the remission of their sins. The whole sermon was delivered without a trace of hesitation or fear and with a power that was obviously supernatural in its effect upon the hearers. The crowd stood in stunned silence, some of them weeping. Conviction of truth and guilt was overwhelming. Peter was conscious that the Holy Spirit was not only in him, but also in the truth that he was preaching. Jesus had called their new comforter, "The Spirit of truth". A new life had come to both preacher and sermon, a combination that would change the world.

Peter stood and wept that day of Pentecost, as a total of three thousand people repented and were baptised and added to the church at Jerusalem. They worked late into the evening dealing with the people who wanted to get right with God. It was awesome! Many wonderful signs and miracles were done in the name of Jesus and the praises of the grateful people rose to the throne of the Almighty.

In the following weeks many converts were added daily to the church. Thousands were brought to Christ and sick bodies were healed. This is what it had all been for! The years of preparation, discipline and suffering, were all for this. Now it was their responsibility to take it to the world.

Peter walked alone, out into the city. It was late and he lifted his eyes to the night sky and shed tears of gratitude. He talked with his absent friend, although he knew that He was not really absent. It was just that he could not see Him anymore.

"Wherever you are Lord Jesus, wherever that place called heaven is, that you ascended to, I know that you can hear me talking to you, and I want to thank you for everything. Thank you for calling me from the fishing boats, and thank you for teaching me the lessons which I needed to learn, even when you spoke harshly to me, and thank you for helping me to believe, when I found it so difficult. Thank you for praying for me and forgiving me when I failed you so badly. Thank you for dying for me on Golgotha's cross and paying the price for all my sin. And thank you for returning to the Father, and thank you for sending the Holy Spirit. Thank you for allowing me to be your servant. Help me now to truly be a rock in your Kingdom. Help me to be a fisher of men."

CHAPTER TEN

"Bury me beneath your sea of hate,
And seek to quench the liberating torch I hold;
But I will surely rise from hells domain,
To hold aloft unquenched truth again"

A WEAK EARLY-MORNING SUN WASHED THE rooftops of a peaceful looking Jerusalem in its cool, but complimentary light. The city of memories, globally unique, predestined to dominate world history both in time and eternity, lay in feigned passivity at the beginning of another day. Herod's temple stood proud and silent on Mount Moriah, its marble pinnacles and golden domes reflecting the first rays of the sun in a dazzling, fiery beauty, which qualified it to be the symbol of the ownership of this city by the God of Abraham, Isaac and Jacob. The sun was pouring pools of light onto the patchwork of rooftops, compelling the early morning traveller from the Olivet descent, to avert his gaze from the brightness of the spectacle. Such was the magnificence of the city, which the Great Creator chose, from all the cities of the world, as the location of His name. He called it Jerusalem, "Habitation of Peace", although it was destined to be the bloodiest city on earth.

Today was no exception to the enigma. Beneath the cloak of apparent tranquillity and peace, thoughts of anger and violence filled the heart of Annas, son of Seth, high priest of Israel and honoured president of the supreme council of the Jewish people, commonly known as the Sanhedrin. He was appointed to his lofty office by Quirinus, the imperial governor of Syria, in AD 7. Forced to surrender his title by Valerius Gratus, procurator of Judea in AD 14 to one Ismael, son of Phabi, he succeeded, in all but name, to continue to be the power behind the throne. When his son-in-law, Joseph Caiaphas, became high priest some eleven years later, Annas strengthened his hold still further, assuming once more the co-title of high priest. As president of the Sanhedrin, he was a man of considerable influence and power.

He took his seat as chairman at the head of the semi-circular council chamber and ran a troubled eye over the assembled senate. They were all there, the captain of the temple, the chief priests, the scribes and lawyers, elders and rulers of the people, all that were necessary to convene the session as a supreme court of law, with power to pass both judgement and sentence, even the ultimate penalty of death. A murmur of restrained conversation filled the chamber. This was not a scheduled meeting of the council, hence the unusually early start, but a rather hastily called assembly, to deal with a most pressing and urgent case of subversive behaviour, on the part of one Simon bar Jonas, generally known as Simon Peter, and his accomplices.

This was not the first time that the Galilean radical had been summoned to appear before them. Ever since the crucifixion of Jesus of Nazareth and the strange happenings on the day of Pentecost this man Peter had filled Jerusalem with his doctrines. The whole city was ablaze with the new religion and many thousands of adherents now claimed to follow Jesus and proclaimed Him to be the Jewish Messiah. The scheme of Annas and Caiaphas, to remove the threat which Jesus posed to Judaism, by killing Him, had blown up in their faces. The church in Jerusalem was growing by the day and this accursed Peter was laying the blame for the crucifixion of Jesus, very much at the door of the Jewish leaders, especially Annas and Caiaphas, as they were directly involved in His arrest and subsequent judgement. His emotive teaching was having a dramatic effect and was undermining their authority over the people. The council was in no doubt, that both he and his colleagues should be stopped, but how to accomplish such an end was both delicate and difficult. The effect of the Jesus teaching was being enhanced by some undoubted displays of supernatural power, which was very attractive to the general populous. Annas was angry, perplexed and more than a little frustrated.

The officers had been dispatched to bring the prisoners from the common prison, where they had been incarcerated the previous day. Annas waited nervously. The senate would expect a lead from him and he was by no means sure what he should do. He cast his eye over the paperwork containing the report of the previous hearing, more to avoid the gaze of his peers than from any real necessity to read it, for the details were very clear in his mind. The situation, he recalled, had taken a very serious turn, with the case of the healing of the crippled man at the temple gate.

The man in question was in his early forties and had been lame from birth. It was common knowledge, that every day, a group of loyal friends, carried the poor man to the same place in the temple, to enable him to support his meagre existence, by begging from the religious people as they passed through.

They caringly positioned him on a rough woven mat, to alleviate his discomfort whilst sitting on the cold stone floor and there he was left to plead alms from the more fortunate visitors to the temple. He became a well known figure by reason of the fact that he daily occupied the same well traversed position at the side of the gate called Beautiful. The gate was so called because of its breathtaking ornate beauty, without doubt the most magnificent of the numerous gates within the temple courts. Beyond the golden grapevine, which drooped with resplendent grace from the lofty arch, was the sacred altar of burnt offering, a symbol of sacrifice, atonement and intercession. And here the beggar sat, within sight of that symbol, now fulfilled by the atoning death of Jesus Christ, but ignorant of the meaning of that fulfilment. How could he understand unless someone explain it to him? Unrecognised by the Jewish world and its religious leaders, the great sacrificial lamb had shed His blood and paid the final price for all man's sin on the naked, rocky hill called Golgotha. This altar of Levitical law, within the temple in Jerusalem, was only a symbol of the true sacrifice, a sacrifice which had paid for the miracle which was now to take place within its shadow.

Many times in previous months Simon Peter and his friend John, even Jesus Himself, passed by the cripple at the gate, usually pausing to give to him the alms for which he begged. Today, true to their custom, but now without their Master, the two friends made their way to the temple at the hour of prayer. Peter was conscious of a strange feeling of inexplicable excitement stirring in his spirit. Since the wonderful happenings in the upper room on the day of Pentecost he felt so different, as though a new power was generated in his spirit, a fresh and living expectation, bubbling like a spring deep within. His step quickened as they neared the magnificent Gate Beautiful and he felt drawn to the beggar cripple whom he had seen so many times before. He glanced a little pensively towards his friend, hesitated for a moment at the steps, and then navigated his path through the passing throng until he stood, trembling slightly, before the pathetic figure which crouched, hunched and withered, at his feet. John also found a place at Peter's side and the two friends, closer than brothers, were simultaneously moved with compassion. So many times they had stood alongside Jesus as He presented Himself before the needy, but this time they were without the physical presence of their Lord.

"Look on us," Peter said.

That was all he said, and the man's despairing eyes were slowly, hopelessly lifted to meet the eyes of these servants of the Lord Jesus. A smile weakly crossed his dulled countenance in expectation of a gift. It was not usual for his benefactors to take the time to speak to him. They normally just dropped him a coin as they passed. He lifted his begging bowl with no more eagerness than normal, but then felt the sting of disappointment as the man before him spoke again.

"Silver and gold have I none," he said.

So he was to receive nothing after all. He lowered his bowl and looked down at his twisted legs again.

"But such as I have, give I thee."

He did not understand the meaning of the man's words, but, in a moment, anticipation replaced his disappointment. A peculiar thrill of exhilaration passed through his body.

"Silver and gold have I none; but such as I have give I unto thee: In the name of Jesus Christ of Nazareth rise up and walk."

Peter was taken aback by his own boldness. What kind of inspiration, confidence, or faith, was inciting him to make such an unlikely declaration? How could he, a lowly Galilean fisherman, command a man to walk who was born a cripple? Yet at the same time he felt calmly certain. There was no doubt, just a knowledge, tempered in the furnace of affliction and discipline, finally perfected by his dismal failure and subsequent repentance and restoration. Peter knew the Spirit of Christ and believed in the authority of His name. The power that came upon him at Pentecost was now the silent, controlling influence in His life. He knew that this poor cripple was going to walk. He was possessed of an overwhelming confidence in the power of the name of Jesus, which made him feel as though he was by-passing the man's natural ears and speaking directly to his spirit. Peter was merely the vehicle, the voice, by which Christ Himself was commanding every natural law, and everything that was humanly impossible, to submit to the will of God. God was commanding the cripple to walk! Peter was not merely hoping for a miracle. He was not just stabbing in the dark. The spiritual man was being controlled by the Holy Spirit, defying all human logic, usurping every negative assertion, and embracing the miracle.

It all happened in an instant! The lame man felt the power of Peter's words reverberate through his body, whilst at the same moment the strong hand of the fisherman was gripping his and urging him to his feet. He surrendered to the helping hand and the power of the Holy Spirit swept through his frame. His feet and ankle bones pulsated with feeling and strength for the first time in his life. Suddenly he could move his legs! He leaped to his feet and began to walk. He had never walked before and now he could walk! Onlookers were screaming with excitement, but his own voice rose above them all. He leaped and danced and shouted. He wanted the whole world to know that he could walk. Then he was running, deeper into the temple, still shouting, jumping, and slapping his legs. The crowd stood back, astonished. They knew this beggar man, who sat for so many years at the gate Beautiful and they were filled with wonderment at the miracle which they now witnessed. A great crowd gathered in the area of the temple known as Solomon's porch.

And so it was that Peter preached to the crowd that day in the temple, a powerful and convicting sermon. He assured the people that no mere human power had made this man whole, but the power of the Christ, who they had delivered up so unjustly to be crucified. He accused them of killing the Prince of Life, but at the same time acknowledged their ignorance in committing the crime. He called them to repentance, with the promise that their sins would be forgiven. The crowd continued to grow as Peter preached. The news of the miracle was spreading with the passing of every minute and multitudes came and were deeply affected by the words they heard. Nobody could deny that an awesome miracle had taken place and now that miracle paved the way for truth to be declared and received.

Peter was still preaching when the delegation of temple priests, accompanied by the temple ruler and a group of Sadducees, pushed their way through the excited crowds to apprehend the perpetrators of such an unprecedented disturbance. Much to the displeasure of the people, the apostles were arrested and escorted from the temple and taken to the common prison, where they were to spend the rest of the evening and night. Tomorrow, Peter would preach again, to a very different kind of congregation, to the august and hostile company of elders and priests which made up the Jewish council known as the Sanhedrin. Meanwhile Jerusalem was shaking. Thousands were giving glory to God for an undeniable miracle and the story of Peter's pronouncement over the man in the name of Jesus of Nazareth was being told and retold throughout the city. Peter and John laid their heads on the hard floor of their cell that night, uncomfortable and cold, but inside, burning with joy and thankfulness, for all that the Lord had done, completely unaware that the church in Jerusalem had grown by thousands more.

Annas ran a weary hand across his forehead, and then thoughtfully stroked his greying beard. He mused upon the impact that Peter's address had made upon the council on the morning after the beggar's healing. He had forthrightly accused the religious leaders, no holds barred, of the crucifixion of Jesus of Nazareth, but then proclaimed Him to be the healer of the man at the gate of the temple. The apostles actually produced the restored cripple in court and had him testify to the validity of the miracle. The senate marvelled at the fearless boldness of their prisoners and retired into private session to discuss the matter and devise a scheme to limit the spread and influence of their teaching. They privately acknowledged the reality of the miracle and were troubled at the authority and recognition it apparently gave to Peter and John. They felt powerless to presently take any serious action, because of the widespread public opinion and agreed to instruct them to immediately cease preaching in the name of Jesus, on pain of punishment if they disobeyed. They did this, but, to their horror, Peter responded with undaunted courage and his reply was almost insolent.

"Whether it be right in the sight of God to hearken to you more than unto God, judge ye. For we cannot but speak the things which we have seen and heard."

So it had progressed from there. They reluctantly allowed the preachers to walk free and news of more miracles became a daily annoyance. Signs and wonders were taking place at the hands of these men, which in many people's eyes were indisputable demonstrations of divine power. Solomon's porch became the scene of numerous healings as Peter and his fellow apostles continued to preach Jesus Christ. People began bringing their sick into Jerusalem from outlying towns and villages, in the hope that Peter would pray over the broken bodies of their loved ones and friends, in the name of Jesus. They even laid their sick in the streets, where they thought that Peter would be passing by, so that the shadow of the servant of Jesus would fall across them. So close was his walk with God and so simple and quickened was their faith, that many received miracles of healing in this manner and departed Jerusalem to tell others of the wondrous things that were taking place. As far as Annas was concerned this whole series of events had now reached frightening proportions and the Sanhedrin was losing its grip. Something had to be done. The problem was that he had no idea what to do. He was worried now, in case his indignation and fear had run ahead of wisdom. He had impetuously issued a warrant for the arrest of the preachers and thrown them once more into prison, without really thinking through what long term action could be enforced. In a few minutes his two enemies would once more be standing before the council and the dilemma facing the

Sanhedrin remained unchanged. How could they possibly end the activity of these men, without causing an uprising amongst the general population?

The high priest called the senate to order as the captain of the guard appeared, somewhat nervously, at the council chamber doors. Annas spoke sharply.

"Well, bring in the prisoners!"

The captain moved forward and took up a position in the centre of the chamber, at all times keeping his eyes fixed unwaveringly on the face of the priest. He steadied himself and took a deep breath.

"Sir," he said, "we do not have the prisoners. We went to the prison, as you commanded us. The guard was in position at the gate and the prison doors were locked and secure. We explained the purpose of our mission and were immediately given access to the cells to secure the prisoners."

The captain paused annoyingly and drew another deep breath.

"Sir," he said, "There were no prisoners in the cell. They had disappeared. We searched sir, but they were definitely not there."

His voice had fallen to a faint whisper.

"Sir," he murmured, apologetically, lowering his fear-filled eyes, "it's a miracle!"

The entire Sanhedrin sat in stunned silence. No-one spoke. Annas slowly, very slowly, lowered his head and then, just as slowly, raised it again. He opened his hands in a plaintive gesture of resignation and asked, "Where will all this end?" He asked the question to himself but in the hearing of them all. Nobody ventured an answer and silence reigned. The embarrassment of the court was eventually alleviated by the arrival of a flustered looking messenger, who had obviously been running. His face was red from exertion and his hair was wet with perspiration. He burst into the assembly without regard for decorum or ceremony.

"The men that you put in prison sir, they are in the temple. They are stood teaching the people about Jesus of Nazareth and huge crowds are listening to them. I can show you where they are if you wish."

He was a man short in stature. He now straightened himself to full height, folded his arms in front of him in a gesture of triumphant pride, and waited for instructions. A hubbub of noisy conversation filled the room. Annas lifted his hand in a plea for silence.

"Captain, go and bring these men here, but carefully. We do want to stir up an insurrection of the people. These men have become popular, so use no violence; just bring them to me."

Again, his tone was weary and his heart was troubled. And now they must wait longer. He attempted a weak smile and a buzz of conversation relieved the tension in the chamber.

Peter and John and their accompanying guard arrived at the senate amazingly quickly. The prisoners had offered no resistance. To the contrary, they appeared almost eager for the proposed interview with Annas. They were positioned appropriately before the court and challenged by the high priest to answer for their continued disobedience to the edict previously issued, barring them from preaching in the name of Jesus. There was significantly no mention of, or question relating to, their escape from the prison and the mystery of the locked doors. Annas wanted no stories of angelic rescue missions at this juncture in proceedings. The problem was complex enough as it was.

Peter stepped forward two paces to command the floor. His naturally ruddy face was glowing with elation and passion. He felt no fear and exhibited none. His eyes were on fire. His voice was powerful, but controlled. What a difference from the coward who had wilted and lied before these very same people on the night of the Lord's betrayal. He looked straight at Annas.

"We ought to obey God rather than men. The God of our fathers raised up Jesus who you slew and hanged on a tree. Him hath God exalted with His right hand to be a prince and a Saviour, for to give repentance to Israel and forgiveness of sins. And we are His witnesses of these things, and so is also the Holy Ghost, whom God hath given to them that obey Him."

He stepped back and with piercing eyes fearlessly, but calmly, held the gaze of the priest, waiting for his response to the anointed truth. The lawyers, elders and rulers of the people were inflamed with fury; full of murderous intent. They began shouting and hurling abuse at Peter and John and the cry went up demanding that they should be stoned to death. The hall erupted into unseemly scenes of failed tempers and verbal abuse. Had it not been for the intervention of a highly respected Pharisee and doctor of the law by the name of Gamaliel, there was a very serious risk to the lives of God's servants. Gamaliel stood forward and lifted both arms in a plea for order. Slowly the volume subsided and silence reigned.

"Ye men of Israel, men of Israel, calm yourselves."

His voice was both commanding and chiding. He turned and addressed the guard.

"Remove the prisoners; we will discuss this matter privately."

He waited, still standing, until the apostles had been escorted into an adjoining room.

"Ye men of Israel," his voice was now gentle and appealing, "take heed to yourselves what ye intend to do as touching these men. For before these days rose up Theudas, boasting himself to be somebody, to whom a number of men, about four hundred, joined themselves: who was slain; and all, as many as obeyed him, were scattered and brought to nought. After this rose up Judas of Galilee in the days of the taxing, and drew away much people after him: he also perished; and all, even as many as obeyed him, were dispersed. And now I say unto you, refrain from these men, and let them alone: for if this counsel or this work be of men, it will come to nought: but if it be of God, ye cannot overthrow it; lest haply ye be found even to fight against God."

Gamaliel's short speech had a remarkable effect upon his learned colleagues. First one, and then another, gave support to his wise counsel and it was agreed that once again the offenders be charged to keep their silence and then be freed. This time, however, the threat would be accompanied by a flogging.

Peter and John were deliberately humiliated before the seventy one members of the Sanhedrin. Servants were ordered to carry into the chamber a crudely built wooden frame, which was carried into the centre of the hall. Peter and John were then stripped naked and fastened by their hands and feet to the whipping frame and a rough, flexible rod, was laid time and time again across their naked flesh. First huge welts appeared, but then the flesh began to split and the blood ran hot across the stinging, stripped skin. They did not cry out, or in any way show weakness and, fortunately, Annas called a halt to the public torture, before unconsciousness could intervene. Gamaliel bowed his head in shame and hoped against hope that these men were not of God.

An hour later the two friends staggered from the presence of the council into the busy street, rejoicing that they were able to suffer shame for the name of Jesus. The pain was horrendous and they were destined to carry the scars of their beating for the rest of their lives, but it was nothing compared with all that Jesus had suffered for them. Peter's body burned with pain and his legs felt weak beneath him, but his heart glowed with love. This time there was no need for bitter tears of regret for denying his friend. He glanced heavenward and sensed the Saviour's smile. He gently touched the arm of Zebedee's son.

"Tomorrow John, you and I will go fishing," he paused before adding, "For men."

John smiled through the pain which had sucked the colour from his cheeks.

"And tomorrow Peter, the Lord will confirm His word with more miracles!"

CHAPTER ELEVEN

"Do none exist who are beyond loves reach;
None too perverse to know His pardoning touch?
Can he whose hands left Christians dead,
Forgiveness find, the Gospel spread?"

MUCH TO THE CONSTERNATION AND frustration of Annas and Caiaphas, the cruel flogging to which they subjected Peter and John made not the slightest difference. Undeterred, they continued to fill Jerusalem with their doctrine and daily frequented the temple and different houses throughout the city, preaching Jesus Christ. Every day new converts were added to their number. The church was also beginning to organise itself, appointing deacons to care for the widows and the poor and to administer the business side of a growing concern. Amongst these appointees was a man named Stephen who, in addition to his work as a deacon, quickly rose to prominence as a man of outstanding faith and power, performing great wonders and miracles amongst the people, and thereby attracting to himself considerable opposition and hatred. Certain men, of the Synagogue of the Libertines, aided by a number of others, disputed with Stephen and, failing to win the day, hired false witnesses against him, to accuse him of blasphemy against Moses and against God. They so stirred up the people against him that the elders and scribes issued a warrant for his arrest and brought him, as they had previously brought Peter and John, before the Sanhedrin. The charges relating to blasphemy were officially read out.

Stephen's reply to the council was an eloquent and powerful summary of Jewish history from Abraham to Joseph, then from Moses to the time of Christ. He skilfully showed how, throughout their history, the people had rebelled against God's will, rejecting Moses and persecuting the prophets. He concluded a quite lengthy oration by denouncing the present system and accusing its leaders of being no better than their forefathers, by betraying and murdering Jesus Christ. The members of the Sanhedrin were furious! The room was filled with hissing hatred and unashamed demands for his death. The noise rose to an unseemly roar and dignity and order were abandoned as they mobbed Stephen, who stood with eyes uplifted to the heavens and declared, "Behold I see the heavens opened, and the Son of Man standing on the right hand of God."

Nothing could have been designed to aggravate the anger of his enemies more than this, a statement which, in their opinion, was confirmation of his guilt and blasphemy. They leapt from their seats, shaking their fists and screaming for his blood. They seized God's servant like a pack of hungry wolves, unceremoniously dragging him into the street in full view of the people. The crowds stood back in shocked disbelief at the scene of uncontrolled fury which poured from the house of judgement. Stephen was hurried down the slope, half carried, half pushed, until they reached the rock-strewn Kidron valley. Here, overlooked by the Mount of Olives and the garden where the Lord had prayed on the night of His betrayal, he was viciously murdered. They stoned him to death, gloating over every view of fresh blood and every new wound they opened up. As for Stephen, inspired by the vision of his Lord standing to receive him, he knelt in sweet submission and offered his spirit into the care of the Lord Jesus. His last words, "Lord, lay not this sin to their charge" demonstrated the sincere Christ-like spirit of forgiveness which Stephen always portrayed, but also burned like fire into the conscience of a Pharisee named Saul, who, with callous indifference, was holding the coats of the killers. He was a cold, calculating enemy of Jesus Christ and of all who followed Him. He was a man with much blood already on his hands and one who stopped at nothing to apprehend the hated Christians, zealously raiding their homes, committing them to prison and having many of them put to death. Stephen's final prayer went like an arrow into his heart. No longer an unconcerned onlooker, he was intrigued by whatever strange influence and power could cause a dying man to sincerely seek the pardon of those who put him to death. From that moment the Pharisee became a troubled young man.

The following weeks saw Saul more furiously persecuting the church. He tried to quieten his noisy conscience with more aggressive behaviour, but he was haunted by the dying prayer of Christianity's first martyr, its words pricking and prodding at his guilty heart with supernatural persistence. Soon he was destined to yield to conviction in one of the most amazing conversions in the entire history of the church and become, arguably, its greatest apostle. Logic may ask why God allowed Stephen to die, but the fact is that his premature death gave to the world one of the most effective preachers of all time.

Following the murder of Stephen, all hell broke loose against the church in Jerusalem. Beatings and imprisonments, torture and killing, all became commonplace. Many Christians literally ran for their lives, leaving Jerusalem and heading out into the towns and cities of Judea and Samaria. They did, however, continue to preach Christ, so, wherever they went, the Gospel was spread. The persecution which was designed to crush God's people and annihilate the church, actually caused it to flourish, both numerically and geographically. Before his conversion, Saul of Tarsus widened his area of hostile activity and began to pursue the followers of Jesus into other towns and villages. His name was universally feared throughout every community where Christians met together.

Peter was appalled at the wicked killing of his friend Stephen, whilst at the same time being deeply moved by the account of the wonderful example of forgiveness and love which he displayed in his dying. Indignation burned in his belly at the activities of the evil Saul of Tarsus and the wider persecution which his activities had promoted. Nevertheless, since Pentecost he had become the eternal optimist and no amount of opposition or persecution was going to prevent him from doing God's will. Samaria had received the Gospel through the preaching of Philip the evangelist and the most wonderful demonstrations of the power of the Holy Spirit were taking place. News of miracles of healing and deliverance from unclean spirits was flooding the area with joyful expectation and the elders at Jerusalem felt that Philip was in need of help. Peter and John were duly dispatched to minister into the situation and as they laid hands on the converts, they immediately received the baptism of the Holy Ghost. Everywhere, the church was thriving and growing, feeding on opposition and affliction, carrying its cross with dignity and experiencing the power of Christ's resurrection.

Peter was full of praise and gratitude to his Lord, astonished at His wisdom and at the masterful manner in which He used the enemies of the church to multiply it. Then came the most shocking and unbelievable news that he would ever hear. A rumour had reached Jerusalem that Saul of Tarsus himself had been converted to Christ and was actually testifying concerning Jesus in the synagogue at Damascus, proclaiming Him to be the Son of God. He found it difficult to believe, as did the rest of a very sceptical church. Some very wonderful people were still mourning the loss of their loved ones because of this man's wickedness and now they were expected to believe that he had become a Christian. What new ploy was the scoundrel now engaged in, to destroy God's people? Did he think that he could pretend to be one of them, in order to become a saboteur from within the ranks? Yet as time passed more information came to Peter's attention. It was reported that Saul had actually been on his way to Damascus to imprison Christians, when he was confronted by a vision of Christ, who appeared in the road in front of him in a blaze of glory and struck him blind. It was said that Saul threw himself to his knees as he heard the voice of Jesus and, trembling with fear, asked Him what He wanted him to do. If this story was true, it was the most sensational news!

Peter decided to reserve judgement, but the fact is that, as the weeks progressed there was clear evidence that Saul's activities against the church had ceased. The persecutions appeared to have subsided and nobody seemed to know where Saul of Tarsus was. Rumour had it, that after preaching Christ in the synagogue at Damascus he left the town and headed east towards the desert. He had not been seen since. The church, and Peter, breathed a sigh of relief and thankfulness to God for His mercy and power. Whatever was going on, it was incredible and undoubtedly a most notable miracle had taken place.

Saul had, in fact, retreated into Arabia to be alone with God and reform his doctrines according to his revelation of Jesus as the Messiah. It was not easy for his enlightened soul to accept the forgiveness which he knew he did not deserve, neither was it easy for him to forgive himself for his cruel crimes against the innocent. The scars of his sin against the church were etched forever on his memory and for the rest of his life he considered himself to be "the chief of sinners and the least of all saints." He did not re-emerge from the wilderness for a full three years.

It was certainly a different Saul of Tarsus who eventually returned to Damascus, to preach the Christ he had previously hated and persecuted. He did so with such power and conviction that the Jews in the city took counsel to kill him. The danger was so real, that it led to his necessary, but ignominious escape, by being lowered from the city wall at dead of night, in a basket. He then headed for Jerusalem to face the memories of past misdemeanours and misdirected fervour. With a thankful heart he passed the place on the road where he met the resurrected Christ in such dramatic fashion three years before, pausing for several minutes at the site where he had knelt in the blazing light of Christ's presence and cried, "Lord, what will you have me to do?"

He sorrowfully walked into the valley where he presided over the murder of Stephen and remembered once more how his face glowed like the face of an angel. He could still hear his gracious words of prayer for the forgiveness of his persecutors. He stood and wept where God's servant had stained the ground with his blood and whispered "Sorry Lord and sorry Stephen," to the open heavens. He turned and climbed the hill into the city. Jerusalem now represented the very opposite of that which once dominated his life. It was no longer the symbol of the dead religion of the law, but the city where the Lord Jesus gave Himself as a sacrifice for the sins of the world and brought the law to fulfilment. He was looking for the apostles, with the intention of offering his services to the church, but, despite the passing of the years, fear still gendered caution concerning this notorious convert and it fell to Peter to offer him hospitality. James, the younger brother of Jesus, agreed to meet him, but the rest refused to accept that a man like him could ever change.

Peter and Joanna received Saul warmly into their humble home and he remained with them for fifteen days. Those two weeks were as vital in the preparation of Saul for his future ministry as the three years which he spent in the wilderness. They talked endlessly of Jesus, what He was like, and all the things that He did. Peter related story after story of the three years that he had spent working alongside Jesus, telling Saul of the countless miracles that He saw Jesus perform, how He was daily moved with compassion because of the needs of the people. Peter took his new friend to Calvary, where they stood together and wept with love and gratitude. Then they were in the empty garden tomb and Peter gave him the account of the moment he entered the grave on resurrection morning and found it empty. He told him of his brief and silent meeting with Jesus in the street. They sat together for a while in the Garden of Gethsemane and Peter confessed to him his dreadful denial of his Lord and shared with Saul his feelings of constant grief and guilt. Saul sobbed as he expressed the burden of guilt that he carried every day concerning the evil he had perpetrated against the church.

They laughed and they cried, late into long nights of fellowship and Peter inspired this ex-Pharisee with visions of the Christ, who Saul only met once, as one born out of due time, on the Damascus Road. When Saul departed Jerusalem for Caesarea and from there went home to Tarsus, it was with a fire burning in his belly which would never be put out. A friendship was forged between two men of different upbringings and backgrounds, a friendship which would last until death, but it was to be another seven years before they met again and then only for a very brief time, at the sad occasion of the execution of James the son of Zebedee and the subsequent imprisonment of Peter. It would then be a further seven years before they were to renew their friendship, when the apostles met at the church Council of Jerusalem.

CHAPTER TWELVE

"Can love and pity be confined,
Restricted to one race or creed?
Does not the cross send out the call,
Come! Mercies price is paid for all?"

THE ROMAN ARMY WAS DIVIDED into legions, each one comprising ten cohorts, each cohort being made up of three bands, and each band was divided into two centuries. Originally a century consisted of literally one hundred soldiers, but, as time passed, it could contain any number from between fifty and one hundred men. A legion therefore contained between three thousand and six thousand soldiers, ideally the latter, but often considerably fewer. The authorities in Rome prescribed six cohorts of the military to the procurators of Judea, five of which were stationed at Caesarea, a maximum of three thousand men.

One of the bands, which consisted exclusively of Italians and was predictably called "The Italian Band," was commanded by two centurions (the name given to an officer in charge of a century) one of whom was called, Cornelius. He was a member of the distinguished Corneli family in Rome and a soldier of considerable distinction. He accomplished fifteen years of military service before his promotion to centurion and was now an experienced soldier of a total of twenty four years service. As a member of the Roman military he was forbidden to marry, but, like many of his contemporaries, he had taken a young Jewish girl as his lover and she had borne him three sons. Although he was a Roman officer, Cornelius was deeply interested in and affected by, the Jewish religion. Since arriving in Israel, his latent curiosity about the existence of a supreme being was fed, both by his common law wife and by his growing understanding of the history and politics of the Jews and he was open to believe. He developed a genuine respect for the God of Abraham, as well as a desire to know Him. He shared this, both with his family and the men who were under his command. He conducted his life with honesty and piety, giving alms to the poor and needy and engaging in regular times of private prayer as he pursued the truth. He nurtured a yearning in his heart for a personal relationship with the creator, which, for some reason, his new found Jewish religion failed to give him. He wanted more.

He took his search for the reality of God seriously, sometimes shutting himself away for hours at a time and calling out to the God he could not see, that He might grant him understanding. It was on such an occasion, in the middle of the afternoon, whilst engaged in a time of prayerful solitude, that he had a most remarkable experience. He was never quite sure whether or not he fell asleep, but his room was suddenly filled with the most incredible presence of purity and the hairs on his arms stood up in recognition of the supernatural. His eyes widened with amazement and fear, as an apparition of breathtaking beauty materialised before him and, what he assumed to be some form of angelic being, stepped towards him, quietly calling his name as he did so. Cornelius fell to his knees. The strong, tough, Roman commander was trembling with fear.

"What is it Lord?" he asked, his voice shaking with apprehension. The visitor from another Kingdom addressed the seeking man with words of reassurance. In a voice which, at the same time, both soothed and demanded respect, he told him that his generosity towards the poor and needy had been noted by the Almighty and that his many prayers had been heard. He instructed him to send emissaries to a place called Joppa, a coastal town about thirty five miles to the south, where they should enquire as to the whereabouts of one Simon, a tanner by trade, who lived in a house overlooking the sea. They would find a man lodging there by the name of Simon Peter, who would be able to tell Cornelius what to do. Cornelius bowed his forehead to the floor and when he raised it again, his visitor had departed. He was alone, but the angel's words were ringing in his ears and an overwhelming sense of excitement flooded his soul. He instantly called for the most trusted soldier in his company and two of his household servants. He relayed to them the words of the angel and dispatched them post haste for Joppa, to find Simon Peter.

Peter was, as usual, about his master's business, enthusiastically preaching the Gospel and healing the sick, moving from town to town with unabated zeal. His passion to win the lost was an uncontainable, burning fire in his soul. Twelve months after his meeting with Paul he visited a group of Christians at Lydda, a town nine miles south west of Joppa, in the direction of Jerusalem, where he met a poor paralysed man by the name of Aeneas, who had been confined to bed for the past eight years. Inspired by the Holy Spirit and demonstrating the same boldness of faith as he did at the Gate Beautiful, Peter announced to the crippled man, "Aeneas, Jesus Christ maketh thee whole." The result was instantaneous! Immediately, life and energy poured through every muscle and sinew of the man's withered frame and, rising up, he began to walk and leap and run. The news of the miracle spread like a fire through the whole community, until Lydda and the whole district of Sharon, in which Lydda was situated, was turned to Christ. The news carried as far as Joppa and the Christians there immediately sent an urgent request, imploring Peter to visit them, in the hope that another miracle would reverse a tragedy which had suddenly struck down one of their faithful disciples.

Her name was Tabitha, otherwise known as Dorcas, a woman of great faith and devotion to God, who showed her faith by her many good works and by giving of alms. She had recently fallen very sick and, to the horror and distress of all who knew her, had subsequently passed away. Her friends tenderly washed her body and laid it in an upper chamber of the house in preparation for burial. It was then that news of the happenings in Lydda reached the group and a messenger was sent to bring Peter to the house without delay.

Simon Peter somewhat nervously agreed to make the journey to Joppa. He prayed as he travelled, for he knew that there was nothing in him that could possibly bring life back to a cold corpse. If ever he needed a powerful visitation of the Holy Spirit, he needed it now. The scene at the house was chaotic. It was full of grieving women, weeping and wailing for the loss of their friend, a situation not easy to control. They did seem somewhat comforted by Peter's arrival, although they showed little confidence or expectation of a miracle. Having calmed themselves, they insisted on showing their visitor the many clothes which

Tabitha had made and folded, ready for their distribution to the poor. They were obviously proud of their departed friend and wished to bestow as much honour on her memory as possible. Peter climbed the steps which led to the chamber where the body lay and quietly, but insistently, ushered the mourners from the room. He gazed with prayerful apprehension at the lifeless form of the woman who had been such a faithful servant of Jesus. The corpse had been washed and anointed ready for burial. He reverently knelt at her side and silently bowed his head. How he needed the power of the Holy Ghost. This was an impossible situation, which could only be changed through the authority of the name of Jesus. He remained in silent prayer, until he was possessed of the same confidence which he had felt when he stood before the man at the Gate Beautiful. He then slowly stood to his feet.

"Tabitha, arise!"

That was all he said. He did not repeat it. He did not become emotional. He just calmly issued the command and waited for the answer. Tears of wonderment flooded his eyes as he watched the colour rising in her cheeks. Her flesh grew warm and her chest began to rise and fall as she began to breathe. Her eyes opened as though she woke from sleep and she pulled herself into a sitting position. Peter offered her his hand and lifted her up. She stood at the side of her bed, as healthy and perfect as though she had never been sick. Peter opened the door, called for her friends to come, and presented her to them, alive. It was a sensation, a miracle of miracles. The women screamed with unrestrained delight and the street sang with praises to God. Within the hour the entire town was informed of the unthinkable happenings at the house of Tabitha and they flocked to hear Peter give

all the glory to the power of Jesus of Nazareth. The gospel
was preached and many people believed in the Lord Jesus.
They pleaded with Peter not to leave and he found himself
unable to desert such a ripened harvest field as this. He
was offered accommodation with a man called Simon, in a
pleasant little spot overlooking the sea. There he remained
for three years, using it as a base for reaching out into the
surrounding areas.

The delegation from the centurion, Cornelius, was
approaching Joppa around noon-time on a hot and sticky
summer's day, as Peter went up onto Simon's flat roof to have
a time of prayer. He was feeling rather hungry and, while
food was being prepared for him, he wisely bought up the
opportunity to spend some time with his Lord. He quietly
knelt before God and thanked Him for all the love and
mercy which was touching so many lives and for the power
through the name of Jesus which was healing the sick. A
beautiful sense of the Divine presence closed in around
him and he began to weep with love and joy and heartfelt
appreciation. He lifted his eyes towards the heavens, but his
tears, conspiring with the heat haze, which rose in spiralling
rivulets of mist from the roof top, hindered his sight of the
natural. Instead he saw with the eyes of his spirit, a vision
which was to change his life yet again. Descending from the
empty firmament above him was a huge white sheet, tied at
the four corners to form a large bag. It was moving as though
it contained some monstrous living creature and Peter, with
some alarm, stood to his feet. The sheet came to rest just a
few strides away from him and he saw that it contained,
not one creature, but many. It was heaving with animals;
pigs and creeping things, birds of prey, large and small and
many other living things, which no Jew would ever use for
food. Peter shrank back with horror, repulsed at the very

sight of such a collection of distasteful creatures. Then, to his consternation, he heard the voice of God instructing him, "Rise Peter; kill and eat."

Although not particularly religious in his private beliefs as a young man, Peter was brought up to observe basic Jewish traditions, including what was kosher to eat and what was regarded as unclean and forbidden. To kill and eat the animals in the sheet would break traditions which were part of his Jewish identity. He could not possibly do it!

"Not so Lord," he said with characteristic boldness. "I have never eaten anything that is common or unclean."

The voice from the heavens came again, this time with a tone of rebuke and command.

"What God hath cleansed, that call not thou common."

Peter was caught between the voice of God and loyalty to religion. To eat these unclean animals felt like a betrayal of his Jewish roots, but not to do it felt like a betrayal of Jesus. He suddenly found himself back at the fire in the judgement hall, denying that he knew Jesus, betraying the One he loved, and he knew what he must do. He trembled at the thought of reliving his mistake. He must not go there again! Tradition or no tradition, he would remain faithful to the God he knew. He stared with amazement at the writhing mass of unpalatable, forbidden livestock and hesitated, trembling with apprehension, afraid to obey, yet knowing he must. Again the voice came, insistent, uncompromising.

"Rise Peter; kill and eat!"

Slowly Peter reached out his shaking arm to take hold of a small dirty looking boar. He felt sick as his hand touched the hairy flesh at the back of its neck. As he did so the sheet began to move. It was being raised by some powerful, unseen hand, and within seconds Peter was able to walk underneath it. It rose like a huge balloon into the sky and disappeared into the blaze of the midday sun. The vision was over and Peter slumped to the floor, rubbing his eyes and forehead. He remained there for several minutes, musing over the strange apparition he had seen. He prayed in his confusion, that God would show him the meaning of his perplexing vision. Instead of receiving an explanation, he heard the voice of the Holy Spirit speaking in his mind.

"Behold, three men seek thee. Arise therefore, and get thee down, and go with them, doubting nothing: for I have sent them."

As Peter made his way down from the roof, a servant of the household was ascending the steps with a message for the preacher. Three men were at the door and were asking to speak with him.

So it was that Peter sat and listened to the story of the angelic visitation experienced by Cornelius and how he had been instructed to send for Simon Peter. As he listened, the meaning of his own vision of the sheet and the unclean animals became clear to him. He was being asked to go and share the gospel with a foreigner, a man who was not a Jew, something which had not been done before. If Jesus was the Jewish Messiah, then surely the message that He brought was for the Jews. He was, of course, overlooking the fact that the Jews had rejected their Messiah and put Him on a cross, which now made it possible for all people, Jews and Gentiles, to find salvation. Because of God's promise to Abraham, the Jewish people considered that they were special, of greater importance than the rest of the world, and looked down upon the Gentiles as unclean. The realisation that, through his vision, God was showing him that they were neither unclean nor outside the boundaries of His love, swept over him like a tidal wave. In the vision he was commanded to abandon a life-long tradition and eat the unthinkable. The meaning was clear. He was to abandon his religious and cultural bias against non-Jews and carry the gospel message to a Roman centurion. He determined to stride across the line from the presumed Jewish ownership of Christ and offer Him to the world. Peter and his host, Simon the Tanner, invited their visitors to lodge with them for the night, thus breaking Jewish tradition. They made them comfortable and poured upon them the hospitality of those touched by the love of Jesus. The following morning they embarked on the journey northward to Caesarea.

It was not the first time that Peter had visited the impressive city, with its superb mix of architecture, culture and trade. The two-part, deep-sea harbour, named Sebastos (Greek for Augustus) by its architect Herod the Great, in honour of Emperor Augustus, imposed itself on the spectacular exit to the Mediterranean Sea, and the ingenious aqueduct, magnificent amphitheatre, and 20,000 seat hippodrome, attracted a cosmopolitan population numbering 100,000 people. Its wide roads, ornate temples, the palace of Pontius Pilate, with its elaborate facade, the Roman baths, colourful market, theatre productions and sporting events, made it the most important and sought after city in Israel, second only to Jerusalem. His heart quickened a pace as he approached the military quarters. He had never been this close to the domain of Rome, let alone actually entering the accommodation of one of its officers. His escort opened to him instant access to an area which otherwise would have been forbidden to him. It was another world from the one he knew, the opposite pole from his humble abode in Capernaum. He was shown through grand corridors, into a spacious Atrium complete with marble columns and soft couches. Through an opening at the far end of the chamber, provided with curtains which were rarely used, he could see the Tabilnum, where Cornelius stored the family valuables, and beyond it, the courtyard, which the Romans called the peristyle. Peter's eyes scanned the Atrium. The room was full of people, the entire membership of Cornelius' family, together with his close friends, all of whom had been invited to listen to the ordinary looking Jew, who now stood before them.

The centurion rose with undisguised excitement as Peter entered the room, stepped forward and greeted him with an astonishing display of homage. He humbly knelt at the feet of the Galilean, in an act of reverent worship. For a moment Peter was speechless with surprise, but then wasted no time in urging his host to rise, assuring him that he was just another mere mortal and in no way someone to be worshipped. Cornelius obediently stood to his feet. He was a tall man in his early forties and was wearing a knee length white tunic underneath a black leather cuirass. A red cape, fastened at the shoulders, fell to just below the knee. He wore a shoulder sheath for his absent sword, arm bands and calf bands, but no hat and was shod with a pair of slip-on sandals. He was a handsome man with a weatherworn look to his strong square features. His clean shaven face sported a knife scar across his chin, a constant reminder of how perilously close he once came to death. The muscles in his shoulders, legs and arms displayed his physical fitness.

His eyes were strangely gentle for a man of his occupation and his expression was one of genuine humility. He politely introduced Peter to his partner, Julia, who was a woman of considerable beauty and almost as tall as her lover. She was blessed with long black hair, which she wore without adornment and which was left to fall freely down her back. She had eyes to match. Like Cornelius, she also wore a white tunic, but her outer garment was a short sleeved stola, open from the shoulders to the waist and secured at the shoulders by a pair of ornate broaches. Her feet were dressed with elaborately embroidered slippers. Her face shone with warmth as she smiled her greetings to the stranger. She gave a shallow curtsey and said, "Salve" (meaning "good health"). Without understanding the meaning, Peter also smiled and repeated the greeting. He then became conscious that every eye was upon him and waiting for him to speak.

Peter stood in strange contrast to his surroundings. His ruddy face, full beard and plain clothes set him apart from his somewhat august audience. With an opening of his hands in a gesture of apologetic reticence, he explained that this was the first time that he had been in the dwelling of a citizen of Rome. He was, in fact, yet again breaking Jewish convention by being in the home of a Gentile, but he told the story of his vision and how God had made it clear to him that he must not regard any as beneath him, or beyond the love of the Creator. He had been instructed by a power far superior to Jewish tradition, to presence himself in the home of Cornelius on this occasion. His host then eloquently gave his own account of the visit of the angel to his room and how he was given Peter's exact whereabouts and instructed to send for him and request his help. A buzz of excitement spread across the room as those present realised that this interview was so amazingly ordained by some divine power, who had communicated with both parties in order to bring them together. Peter then preached Christ to them. All nervousness gone, he launched into the history of the Gospel, beginning with John the Baptist and the ensuing ministry of Jesus of Nazareth, how He healed the sick and cast out devils, died on a cross and was raised again on the third day. He explained how he and the rest of the disciples were commanded to preach the Gospel, with the promise that whoever believed would receive forgiveness of sins.

The atmosphere in the house of Cornelius became charged with the presence of the Holy Spirit. His wide-eyed listeners drank in the truth with an eagerness and hunger Peter had rarely seen. They were so open to receive, so moved by his words, that Peter's spirit trembled with joy and anticipation. The truth was sinking deep into the hearts of these Gentiles. Some of them were visibly moved, tears were flowing, and some were falling to their knees before the Lord. Peter continued to preach and, while he did so, the power of the Holy Spirit came upon the assembled company in a similar way that it did on the day of Pentecost and the room was filled with the music of praise, pouring from Roman lips, in languages they had never learned. It was awesome! Peter knelt amongst the family and friends of Cornelius, now his brothers and sisters in Christ, and wept with joy as they bathed in the Glory of God. What an amazing turn around! The apostles back in Jerusalem were going to find this one difficult to understand! But deny it, they could not!

Peter reasoned that if God saw fit to baptise these non-Jews with His Spirit, there was no reason why they should not be baptised in water, to seal their allegiance to Christ. So he boldly commanded them to be baptised and they reverently made their way to the Roman baths, where the first Gentile converts were baptised into the name of the Lord Jesus. Following considerable pressure from his new friends, Peter remained with Cornelius and his eager new converts for several days, during which time he taught them many things concerning the Kingdom of God. He told them stories of his time with Jesus, about the many miracles which he had witnessed and the numerous lessons which he and his friends had learned.

As he made his way back to Jerusalem Peter knew that questions were bound to be asked concerning his communication with the Gentile world. It was certainly true that the Jewish Christians had misgivings concerning his contacts with Rome and were waiting to contend with him about what they regarded as a serious deviation from their purposes. They listened, however, to the full account of all the happenings at Caesarea, how Peter came to go there, and how God had baptised the people with the Holy Spirit and it soon became clear to them that God was very much behind the conversion of Cornelius and his company, and that He had used Peter and the thirsty soul of a Roman Centurion, to push open a door, a door to the whole world, which would never again be closed. From that moment the Gospel was available for everybody, Jew or Gentile, and, whoever believed in the power of Christ crucified, would find pardon and peace through the shedding of the blood of Jesus Christ. They were left without argument and enthusiastically joined Peter in thanksgiving and rejoicing, glorifying God because He had also "to the Gentiles granted repentance unto life."

Following his conversion, Cornelius honourably resigned his military commission and married Julia, thus legitimising his domestic relationship before God. He fellowshipped with the local Christians and became an active and passionate preacher of the Gospel. He later became the first Bishop of Caesarea. Following the fire of Rome in 64 AD he made plans to return to Rome to help with the rebuilding programme.

CHAPTER THIRTEEN

"From death's dark jaws and prison's chains,
Deliverance came by angel hands;
To spread my net away from home,
My fishing grounds, the sea of Rome"

IN THE YEAR 44 AD, seven years after his meeting with Saul of Tarsus and three years after the conversion of Cornelius, Herod Agrippa called for the arrest and execution of Simon Peter. On the night before his execution, he slept fitfully in his cell in the fortress Antonia. He was uncomfortably chained to his two guards who snored, unconcernedly, one on each side of him. He was nervous about the events that the morning light would bring. He hoped that, like his friend James, the son of Zebedee, he would die with honour and not in any way disgrace his Lord. He did not feel afraid of dying, but everything seemed surreal and premature. He felt incomplete. He believed that he had so much work to do for Jesus in the world and now it was obviously not going to be accomplished. He thought of how James must have felt the same way and he was now dead. He found some comfort in the thought that soon he would be with him, together in the presence of Jesus, but he ached for his beloved Joanna. She seemed so upset when she left his condemned cell that afternoon. He wanted to comfort her, but she had used her final visit and further opportunity was denied him. Part of him hoped that she would be there in the crowd tomorrow, but part of him hoped that she would not. He yearned for one more smile into her innocent eyes, but he also knew that such a moment would twist the knife of sorrow in her soul. He whispered a prayer for her into the damp darkness of his cell and then fell into another period of unsettled sleep.

He dreamed, as he often did, of the night he denied Jesus. He never thought of it during his waking hours anymore, but somehow, in the vulnerability of sleep, an unknown persecutor often tortured his subconscious mind. He was back in the agony of that dreadful night in the judgement hall, when he swore that he did not know Jesus. The room was hazy with swirling grey smoke and the eyes of the people were bloodshot and wild. In the dark regions of his mind, he heard the cock crow like a hideous monster, its screeching call crashing like hideous laughter over the scene of his betrayal. Then he was out in the street, scraping his face against the rough stone wall until the flesh was torn and the blood ran free. Then he was sobbing his regret to God, pleading for forgiveness, but he could not find Him. He fell forward, but instead of the cold hard cobbles of the street, he found himself falling into a huge black, bottomless pit. Falling, endlessly falling!

Then his dream went into flash-back and he was walking with Jesus into the Garden of Gethsemane. It was dark and the atmosphere was heavy. Jesus was asking him to support Him in prayer. He wanted to help, but he was so tired! He tried to stay awake, but the air was poisoned with sorrow and he breathed lassitude into his soul. He saw himself sleeping! While Jesus struggled alone against the darkness, he slept. He could see drops of blood weeping from the pores on the forehead of his Lord, but he saw himself sleeping. He could hear a voice in the dark distance of his nightmare telling him that he was not worthy of life. He stood alone before a huge white throne. The judge was rising to leave the court. He was sentenced to death for his crime against the Son of God. The voice laughed at his distress, mocking him, "You thought you were forgiven, you fool! There can be no pardon for the slaying of the Christ. It's over Peter! Die! Die! Die!"

Then, he was back in the garden. He saw the Saviour rise from His knees and wipe His bloody brow with His sleeve. He looked calmer now, at peace. He walked across to Peter's sleeping form and gently shook the shoulder of His friend.

"Peter, wake up! Peter, wake up now! You must come with me!"

Peter opened his eyes. He was no longer kneeling in the garden and Jesus was not there. Instead there stood before him the luminous form of an angelic being, like the one that Mary, the mother of Jesus, once told him came to her when she was only fifteen years of age. His cell was gently glowing with the softest, purest light that he had ever seen. The angel was holding his shoulder and calling his name, urging him to stand up without delay. Peter looked at the sleeping soldiers at his side and the chains that fastened him to them, but his visitor again commanded him to stand. As the bewildered apostle struggled to his feet, the chains which bound him fell silently to the floor and, amazingly, the guards slept on.

"Gird thyself, and bind on thy sandals. Cast thy garment about thee and follow me."

Peter obeyed the angel without question, like a man lost in his dream. His eyes were vacant, as though he saw a phantom and followed a vision. The gates of his cell were not locked and the third guard, who kept it, was fast asleep. They exited the inner prison, passed through the outer prison and approached the Iron Gate which led to the city and to freedom. Peter watched through the mist of unreality, as the gate was mysteriously opened by an unseen hand and the two of them walked unchallenged, through the open gates, and down the steps to the deserted street below.

He stood for several minutes like a man in a trance. He wondered when his dream would end. Then he wondered if it was a dream. He turned to speak with the one who had led him to freedom, but he was nowhere to be seen. He was alone and he was outside the prison. He tapped his feet on the stone path and drew the cool night air into his lungs. This was no dream! He was free! It was real! He began to walk away from Antonia, and then he was running. His mind was a whirlpool of thoughts, until wisdom required him to rationalise his position. He stopped and considered where he should go and decided on the house of Mary, the mother of John Mark. It would not be the first place that the authorities would look for him when they mounted their search. He set out at a controlled pace for the home of his friends, offering grateful thanks to God for his deliverance from death.

It was 2am when Peter arrived at the home of his friend John Mark. He knocked at the outer door and, having received no reply, proceeded to knock more loudly. He assumed that the household was sleeping, but the fact was that everyone was very much awake and together with a number of visitors, were engaged in passionate prayer for Peter's deliverance. They had been praying since nightfall that somehow God would send His angel and deliver Peter from prison and from death. They prayed with much fervour and many tears. Passionately leading much of the prayer was a weary, but determined Joanna, pleading with the Almighty for the life of her husband. The cry of intercession rose to a great crescendo of noise as the group reached for God and fought against the powers of darkness. Peter was now banging with some gusto on the door of the heavy wooden gate and becoming a little anxious in case the noise he was creating attracted unwanted attention. Eventually, during a lull in the volume of noise, the distant banging on the door was heard and instant silence reigned over the group of Christians. It was possible that the authorities were rounding up yet more Christian leaders and a sense of fear drove faith from their hearts. Nobody spoke, as a young woman named Rhoda, herself a recent convert through the preaching of Peter, went to the door and called for the identity of the unknown visitor outside.

"It's me, Peter, Simon Peter. Open the door and let me in!"

Rhoda immediately recognised the voice of the man who had led her to Christ and her heart leaped with excitement. The realisation that their prayers were heard and answered sent waves of emotional reactions sweeping through every nerve-end in her body and with a scream of joy she skipped back into the prayer room, shouting that Peter was standing at the door. Her announcement was met initially with bemused astonishment, quickly followed by doubt, scepticism and fear. There was no way that Peter could be at the door. He was in the fortress prison, chained to his guards. This was obviously some hideous plot, hatched by their enemies, to gain access to the house. Joanna stood up. She wanted to go to the door, just in case it was her husband. Rhoda, undeterred by her doubting friends, continued to insist that it was most certainly Peter at the door.

"It must be his ghost."

The speaker was a timid looking man in his twenties. His face was white with fear and his hands were trembling as he interwove his fingers, rocking them from side to side in nervous agitation.

"Perhaps it is," said another. "It is possible that Peter is already dead and that his spirit has come to visit us. We must not open the door!"

Meanwhile the agitated knocking, an expression of mounting indignance as well as urgency, continued unabated and, while the others debated the issue, Rhoda, aided by Joanna, ran to the gate and pulled back the bolts. The door swung open and there he stood, alive and well, flushed with the excitement of his amazing deliverance. Joanna fell into his arms and Peter unashamedly wept as she held him close. Their tears of joy softly watered their kiss of deepest love as they shared their moment of freedom. The astonished prayer group, many of them weeping with gratitude, gathered around and soon they were singing, with a surprising blend of harmonies, the psalm of David which says, "He that dwelleth in the secret place of the most High, shall abide under the shadow of the Almighty ..... Thou shalt not be afraid of the terror by night.... For he shall give his angels charge over thee, to keep thee in all thy ways ...."

Peter assembled the group back in the place of prayer and gave them a full account of his deliverance from the prison. He asked that messengers be sent immediately to James, the brother of Jesus and leading bishop of the church, and to the other apostles, to inform them concerning his safety. He then wisely considered his own position. In a matter of a few hours his disappearance from his cell would be discovered and a city wide search would be launched. If he was to avoid re-arrest and the endangering of all his loved ones, it was essential that he leave town immediately. Joanna wanted to accompany him, but there were natural affairs which needed attention, in addition to which she would slow down Peter's flight and a couple would be more conspicuous than a single man. Peter silently embraced his wife for many minutes and kissed her with the passion of his youth. Then, with a prayer, an exhortation for her to trust the Lord and a promise that he would return for her, he slipped out into the night and, as the first signs of dawn began to wake the world, he made his way beyond the boundaries of Jerusalem. He was heading towards the northwest, but without any fixed destination. He trusted the unseen hand of the One who had opened his prison doors, who, two thousand years before, had guided Abraham from Mesopotamia to Canaan. It was a strange beginning to a ministry which was destined to take Peter across thousands of miles in the cause of his Lord. It was to be a full five years before Peter would return again to Jerusalem.

It is a fact that most fugitives in those perilous days in Palestine fled to the city of Rome for refuge. It was the ideal place to lose oneself, so complex and cosmopolitan was this thriving capital of the world. It was not surprising therefore, that Peter felt drawn in that direction and, after prayerful consideration, headed for the sea port of Joppa. Two days later he took ship for Italy. He watched his beloved Israel disappear behind him and his heart yearned for Joanna. It had been an emotional and hasty parting from his wife and, although she was overjoyed at his escape from prison and from certain death, it was a bitter cup that she was asked to drink as he walked away into the darkness, without any idea of when he might return. Although he sought to shake the memory of her tears from his mind, he felt homesick for her arms. He wanted to walk hand in hand with her by the lake at Capernaum and laugh away the hours, with no thought of politics and religion and death. He lifted his head to the grey skies and once more asked His Lord to comfort her.

It was good to feel the fresh spray blowing in the wind and to once more feel the swaying deck beneath his feet. It was a long time since he had ventured onto the Great Sea and the last time he was on Lake Galilee was on the morning when Jesus made them breakfast and told him to "feed my sheep." He cast the negatives away from his mind and indulged in a smile of pleasure as the rocking ship conjured up fond memories of past fishing escapades with Andrew, James and John. Despite the obvious sadness involved in his flight, he had a powerful sense that he was heading in the right direction, that his destiny had come to birth, that he was at the beginning of his commission to take the Gospel to the world. This did not seem like a mistake or a mere coincidence and certainly not a victory for his enemies. He had a reassuring feeling of vocation and was possessed with knowledge that all was well. And it was. He was bound for Rome, the engine room of the world, the place where he was destined to leave an indelible mark for his Lord and the place to which he would return to die for his Saviour, in fulfilment of the prophesy which Jesus had given to him on that memorable morning on the beach.

He was at sea for a total of three weeks, stopping for a two day layover at Syracuse on the eastern seaboard of Sicily, before passing through the straights of Messina and, hugging the western coast of Italy, finally docking at the city of Puteoli about one hundred and seventy miles south of Rome. He disembarked with a rising tide of excitement. His first sight of this new land took his breath away. The beauty of the landscape around Puteoli was of a kind that he had never witnessed before. His beloved Galilee paled into insignificance before the spectacle of the towering Mount Vesuvius to the east, garlanded to its summit with greenery, poised in the disguise of a motherly guardian above the towns and villages, which naively nestled beneath her skirts, oblivious to the boiling furnace which was building in the belly of this seemingly serene mountain. The richly fertile land to the east of Puteoli was crowded with spectacular villas, the homes of the favoured rich. Peter found himself in a new world indeed, one of the most important commercial ports in the world and the home of the famous Serino aqueduct.

He headed north through the green hills and vineyards, through marshland and rugged, inhospitable terrain, along the Via Campana with its wayside tombs and shrines, stopping for refreshment and sleep at conveniently placed roadside inns. He was fascinated with the endless tide of traffic, from the stately carriages of the wealthy, often pulled by rows of powerful slaves, to the poor, humble carts of the less well off, to the thousands of multi-cultural pedestrians who, as he drew closer to his destination, thronged the access road to this amazing symbol of the ancient world. It was several days after leaving Puteoli that Peter finally reached the outskirts of Rome. His spirit was strangely stirred as he stood on the rise of the hill and gazed across the city which one day would remember and cherish his name, above that of any Caesar. He had never seen this place before, yet he had the feeling that he was arriving home, as if in some peculiar way this city belonged to him and he to it. He felt that he was standing in a special place, at a special moment in history and inexplicable emotion found expression in his tear filled eyes. He shook his head and prepared for the final leg of his journey into the city.

CHAPTER FOURTEEN

"Lead me Lord, to souls oppressed,
To those who languish, void of hope;
I'll sit with them in sorrows night,
Imparting freedom, bearing light"

FROM HIS VANTAGE POINT PETER was able to view the huge sprawling panorama of ancient Rome. She rose like a patchwork blanket from the lowlands, known as the Campagna, which stretched from the sea on one side, to the distant hills on the other. The city appeared to begin from the slope where he now stood, from the villas, houses, gardens and aqueducts which were close at hand, to the ever thickening metropolis which was the disorderly conglomeration of buildings which formed the city of Rome. The view was not as impressive as he had often imagined. His mental picture of Rome was, of course, gleaned from the second hand information which he had been given, added to the limited first hand experiences he had derived from personal contact with Romans back in Palestine. His memories of Caesarea and the house of the centurion, Cornelius, was the backdrop for his imagination and the foundation from which he had built his image of the most powerful city in the world. He expected it to be extravagantly prosperous, highly disciplined, undeniably efficient and, above all, dramatically imposing in its overall appearance. It was a fact that, beneath the cities overall disappointing appearance, the palaces, temples, theatres and gilded baths and facilities did exist, but from where he stood they were lost in the overall picture, alloyed with the crowded hovels of the poor and underprivileged, hidden in the aggregate of rich and poor.

As Peter continued his walk of several miles more into the heart of the city, the roads became even busier, with a blend of military and civilian, rich and poor, Romans and foreigners. He passed beneath a huge aqueduct, one of eleven supplying the city with water, through the arch known as the Porta Capena, and through the Grove and the fountain of Egeria, with its colony of begging Jews. The poor people were dishevelled, diseased and gaunt. They were desperate wrecks of humanity, lost and hopeless. Peter was soon to discover, that there was, in Rome, a Jewish population of more than forty thousand people, most of whom were living in the most appalling conditions in the ghetto known as Transtiberim, a soggy, waterlogged area by the river Tiber, a breeding ground for sickness and disease, which was shunned by all self respecting Romans. This vast harvest field of suffering humanity presented a huge challenge to the man who was to become known as "the apostle to the Jews."

As he approached the city centre he began to taste the atmosphere of Rome. The buildings became more illustrious, more grand and stately. He descended the hill by the Sacer Clivus to the Forum, the hub of Imperial Rome. In front of him was the Capitoline Hill and to his left the Royal Palace of Caesar, with its annexing military quarters, housing the famous Praetorian Guard. It was here that Peter's friend and colleague, Paul, was destined to spend the last days of his life as the prisoner of Jesus Christ. He had nowhere to go in this strange and cluttered city and had very little money left in his purse. He lifted up his heart in prayer for guidance and direction and, ignoring the confusing scenes around him, headed for the river. The centre of Rome was not the place of Peter's calling, but the notorious ghetto of poverty, which awaited him beyond the waterway. Not that Transtiberim was the only poor district in the city, for Rome, like many capitals of today's modern world, was both cosmopolitan and contradictory. The rich and prosperous walked, with callous disregard, amongst the many beggars who occupied public doorways and the steps and vestibules of religious temples.

He hesitatingly traversed the bridge which provided the major thoroughfare from the emperor's palace to the regions beyond the Tiber, noticing as he went the increasing number of Jewish beggars which lined the route. At the far side of the bridge, between the muddy banks of the river and the base of the hill beyond, was an area of flat, damp ground, which was home to thousands of Peter's poverty stricken countrymen. He had arrived at his destination. A vast ocean of broken humanity stretched out across the soggy plain. These people were not oppressed by their Roman masters, just ignored. They were neglected rather than persecuted, left to die like animals. The stench of poverty was overwhelming, nauseating, and, although Peter was no stranger to the poor and humble, it was beyond anything he had witnessed before. Hollow faced children with sunken eyes pulled at his coat. Desperate mothers held dying babies to their dried out breasts. Hopeless men sat idle and lost in the doorways of disease infested hovels. Death glazed the eyes of the living. A lump rose in the throat of the fisherman and a still small voice deep inside his spirit whispered, "Here Peter!" He nodded quietly. He knew! This was the place of his calling. It was to this disgusting and soul destroying slum, that God had appointed him to "feed my sheep." The last words of Jesus rose solemnly in his mind, "Go ye into all the world and make disciples of all nations." This was why He opened Peter's prison doors, saved him from execution at the hands of Herod, preserved him in his journeying and brought him to this place, to a city of the Jews within the walls of Rome, to tell them of the Saviour, to preach hope to the hopeless, to plant a church that would one day touch the whole world.

So Peter did! The fisherman dwelt amongst his fish, giving no consideration to the smell. With the love, care and compassion which had motivated his Master he moved each day amongst these captive Jews and told them, "The Messiah has come." He explained from the historic origins of the Passover lamb, when God delivered ancient Israel from the slavery of Egypt, how Christ, the fulfilment of that Old Testament type, was sacrificed on Golgotha's cross for them all, to deliver them from slavery to sin and give to them eternal life. Wide eyed children listened to his stories of Jesus of Nazareth, as the Galilean fished for souls of every age. He preached Christ to the sick, the cripples and the blind. It seemed a world away from the Gate Beautiful and the abundance of past miracles, but Peter reached for God in his present circumstances. He believed that the past was the forerunner for the present and that there was power in the name of Jesus to heal the sick in Rome, as well as Israel. He began to believe for, and expect, a demonstration of the power of the Holy Spirit right where he was and, immediately, signs and wonders began to attest the preaching of the Gospel. The people began to bring their sick and dying to Peter and multitudes were healed, repented and turned to Jesus. The power of God swept through the needy ghetto and heaven rejoiced that a fire was kindled that would not easily be put out. Christianity had indeed arrived in Rome.

The Jews of the ghetto were not of course the only Jews in Rome, neither were all of Peters fellow countrymen poor. The Jewish community in the city originated with the captives who were brought back from Palestine by Pompey, after his conquest of the Middle East. Their numbers increased with the expansion of trade, resulting in the immigration of a great many rich and prosperous Jews into Italy, including Rome. They practised their religious beliefs quite openly, including the building of Synagogues, enjoying a freedom of expression which was unhindered and undisturbed by the Roman authorities. Rumours and news of astonishing miracles taking place in Transtiberim spread through the Synagogues. The name of Simon Peter, a Galilean recently arrived from Israel, seemed to be on the lips of everybody and the curiosity of the more influential Jews was aroused. Soon Peter found himself ministering during the week to the poor people of the slum and, on the Sabbath days, preaching and teaching in the Synagogues of Rome. He showed them Christ from the books of the law and the prophets, giving personal testimony to the life, death and resurrection of Jesus of Nazareth. Many believed and were saved.

The months passed and evolved into years. Although he was constantly active and poured his life into the people around him, he also experienced times of extreme loneliness. Thoughts of his wife and home often raised a lump in the throat of the man of God and in his weaker moments he succumbed to private weeping. Sometimes, the empty, lost yearning, which we call homesickness, turned into a panic, a stomach turning fear that he might never be able to return to Israel. His heart longed for Jerusalem, for Galilee, for his friends and colleagues, but most of all, for Joanna. But a fire still burned in his spirit. His emotions reached for home, but the spiritual man knew that he was right in the centre of God's purposes. He also knew that the Holy Spirit, who was with him, was with Joanna too and that all was well that was committed into the hands of the Father.

Inevitably problems arose, not from the Romans, who continued to be content to allow the Jews a large measure of religious freedom, but from the Jews themselves. Opposition arose against the teachings of Peter from the Jewish religious leaders, some of whom had heard of the trouble caused by Jesus and His followers to their counterparts back in the home land. The difficulties were initially confined to verbal debate and argument, but as the church took root and began to grow into a more powerful entity, and more and more converts were added daily to the numbers, the situation became more volatile. A riot here and there in the ghetto was ignored, because the city, which was the political and military centre of the world, had more important matters to contend with, but there were limits to Rome's tolerance.

Peter continued to work tirelessly amongst both rich and poor, teaching, preaching and healing the sick. He had considerable boat building skills and, having learned considerably more of the finer points of carpentry from Jesus, he was quite apt at teaching and helping the people to make some improvements to their poorly erected homes and how to build extensions for use as meeting places for the church. The Christians assembled on a regular basis across Transtiberim for the breaking of bread, in memory of Christ's sufferings. They met every first morning of the week, as well as in the evenings for prayer and bible study. Leaders emerged from the people, godly men, who Peter was able to encourage in the care and shepherding of the saints. The church of Jesus Christ was established and, as the years passed, it became a serious threat to Judaism. The Jewish opposition became more organised and the riots became more frequent and violent. Vandalism of Christian meeting places increased to a frightening level and civil disobedience within the ghetto caused the authorities to raise an eyebrow of disapproval. Then Rome raised her fist!

Emperor Claudius reached the end of his patience and ordered the mass deportation of between forty and fifty thousand Jews from Rome. He refused to tolerate anymore the thorn which the Jews had become and, despite the considerable disruption to the cities commerce that he knew it would produce, plus innumerable other inconveniences, he signed the edict ordering their removal. The scenes were unprecedented, as thousands of displaced people, rich and poor, many of them carrying their sick and aged, lined the exit roads from the city. Many of them were destined to die and be buried in shallow road-side graves; others would make it and make homes for themselves in places far away from Rome. Of course the Jews would eventually return and, in the interim, the seeds of the Gospel, which were sown in the hearts of thousands, would be spread across a wider field. When the apostle Paul first arrived in Corinth, Luke records that he found there a certain Jew named Aquila and his wife Priscilla who had recently arrived there from Italy, expelled from Rome under the writ of Claudius. They were already mature followers of the Lord Jesus and of great support to Paul in his ministry.

By the time Claudius issued his command for the eviction of the Jews, news had reached Peter that Herod Agrippa was long since dead and had been replaced by a Roman Procurator, who would have neither memory nor interest in Peter's escape from prison years before. As Peter had to leave Rome like all the other Jews, his mind automatically turned to thoughts of home. If it was right with the Lord he served and there was nothing else planned for his immediate future, he would dearly love to see his wife and the people that he loved. He could practically smell the fish cooking on the open fire behind his house and hear the gentle lapping of the lake against the stones at the water's edge. He could hear Joanna laughing as he lifted her in his strong arms and he could taste the softness of her lips as they found his mouth. He shook himself free from such sweet anticipation and knelt quietly in the presence of His Lord. He was willing, utterly willing, to do His perfect will and to go wherever his sovereign Lord commanded him. He waited for several minutes, listening in prayerful worship. The still small voice smiled its approval. He was free to go home. He stood to his feet with joyful certainty in his heart. He was not just being permitted to return to Israel; this was the perfect will of God.

CHAPTER FIFTEEN

"Teach me to fish where guided,
To be content to serve,
In foreign seas, oft times alone,
Or in calmer waters nearer home"

Peter's return to Israel in 49 AD was a most joyous occasion. He made straight for Galilee and his home at Capernaum, where he knew his wife was living with her aged mother. Joanna had no inkling of his imminent return and so was taken completely by surprise. Their reunion, after so long a separation, was a symphony of screams, laughter and shrieks of delight, interspersed with the soft music of expressed love and complete with interludes of the silence of intimate exchange. Tears of joy and love flowed freely from grateful hearts and they gave united thanks to God for His mercy and protection upon their lives. Their love for the Lord and for each other had grown the more during their years apart, finding depths which defied expression. The next days were days of enjoying each other, exchanging stories, and visiting old friends and neighbours. Peter shared with her the account of his work in Italy and they wept together over the poverty and despair of the people. They spent hours walking, hand in hand, along the lake's narrow beach, or sitting together on the grassy slopes where Jesus had taught the people in His sermon on the mount. Together the happy couple drank in the picturesque beauty of the lake and even took the opportunity to take a boat onto the water. Peter smiled with pleasure as he discovered that old skills never die.

A week later and Peter and Joanna were on their way to Jerusalem. Peter was anxious to see his old friends and receive an update on the growth of the church. What he found produced something of an anticlimax in his spirit. The culture shock was quite overwhelming and everything around him seemed surreal. The situation was not only utterly diverse from the society he had lived amongst in the slums of Rome and had come to regard as normal, but was also different from the conditions which he remembered in Jerusalem. It seemed that everything had changed so much. The church had matured, was more organised, even a little sophisticated and Peter was not sure that he liked the changes. He certainly found it difficult to adjust or fit in with the system of things. In Rome he had operated as he felt was right, as he sought to listen to the voice of God, and his days and nights were filled with ministering and caring for the people who needed his help. In Jerusalem he found them very much occupied in debating doctrines and procedures, arguing about whether Jewish traditions should be observed by Gentile Christians, even whether Gentiles further afield should be compelled to observe such customs. The debate was causing problems between the leaders of the church at Jerusalem and those at Antioch. He was frustrated by what he regarded as unimportant when compared with the needs of humanity, like those he had witnessed in Transtiberim, and he felt out of place, a leader with no-one to lead and nowhere to go.

Before Peter's imprisonment and departure from Jerusalem, when the persecution against the church was at its zenith and Stephen was martyred, many followers of the Lord Jesus fled the city to avoid possible imprisonment and death. Some of them travelled great distances, settling in places as far away as Phenice and Cyprus. The persecution, which appeared at first to be a disaster, served to scatter Christians across thousands of square miles and thereby enhanced the cause of Christ. The fugitive Christians preached the Gospel wherever they went and thousands responded and believed. Eventually a group of believers, native to Cyprus and Cyrene moved to make their homes in Antioch, the capital city of Syria, and a church was born, which was destined to become Jerusalem's most powerful daughter church and the base for the evangelisation of Europe.

When news of the existence and growth of the church at Antioch reached Jerusalem the apostles responded quickly, commissioning Joses Barnabas to visit the church, evaluate its condition and progress, and report back. Barnabas, who had been given his surname by the apostles, a name meaning "son of consolation or exhortation," was a man of unwavering commitment to Christ, having given all that he possessed to the cause of the Kingdom. He was ideally suited for the task and went about his mission with wisdom and genuine humility. He was delighted with what he found at Antioch and was surprised to discover that the majority of people in the church were actually Gentiles. He set about his ministry of exhortation, with Holy Ghost inspired enthusiasm. He preached, encouraged, directed and evangelised, thrilled at the amazing potential which he recognised in this obvious work of God. As a result of his passion and faith, yet more souls were added to the church and the name of Jesus was uplifted and glorified. He felt no inclination to return to

Jerusalem. He was detained by the call of God, which he became convinced was upon this church for future world evangelism, with himself as a part of the plan. Barnabas was a good man, a man of faith and a man of prayer. His faith was firmly rooted in listening to God's voice and waiting for His direction. He learned to operate only on the instructions of his heavenly Father and he lived in quiet submission to the still small voice of the Divine Spirit.

As time passed Barnabas realised that he needed help if the church was going to continue to expand. Logic required that a request be sent to the apostles at Jerusalem that they might send the necessary aid, but, as he prayed, only one name filled his mind, a name long forgotten by most, the name of Saul of Tarsus. Numerous times across any given day Barnabas found his mind full of thoughts of Saul, accompanied by the conviction that the man from Tarsus should be there with him in Antioch. It was now a full ten years since the notorious hater of Christians was converted on the road to Damascus and the buzz of controversy, which greeted his supposed transformation, had long ago ceased to be a topic for debate. He seemed to have disappeared from the scene and the church at Jerusalem was content to let him pass into history. For several days Barnabas thought and prayed and waited, but the name of Saul of Tarsus would not leave his mind. He was constrained to seek him out, find the man who so many had feared and persuade him to return with him to Antioch. After much assuring and reassuring of the church that he would return, Barnabas set out to find the man who, unknown to him, God had chosen to shake the world.

He headed north, rounded the eastern tip of the Mediterranean Sea coast and, following the northern coast westwards into

Cilicia, came to Saul's home town of Tarsus. With some difficulty he eventually located the humble abode, which was the dwelling place of Saul and went to pay him a visit. He knocked gently on a door that had obviously seen better days. He stared absentmindedly at the splitting, dried out timber, as he waited, wondering what kind of a reception he would receive. A bolt was drawn and a tired looking woman in her late thirties partially opened the door.

"I am sorry to disturb you madam," he said hesitatingly, "but I am looking for a man named Saul who, years ago, worked in Jerusalem."

She looked at Barnabas with suspicion, hesitated and then slowly opened the door for him to enter.

"You'd better come in," she muttered, begrudgingly.

She showed Barnabas into a small, dingy room, which was permeated with the lingering odour of damp walls. Without speaking she signalled for him to be seated, left the room and shouted, "Saul, there's somebody here to see you." The atmosphere was not pleasant and Barnabas grew pensive as he waited. Although he had been part of the church in Jerusalem from before the murder of Stephen and was, at that time, a potential victim of Saul's persecution of the followers of Jesus, he had never actually seen him. He began to doubt the wisdom of his visit. He noticed a copy of the Jewish Torah on top of some copious notes on a small table in the corner. Saul was obviously a student of the scriptures.

"Can I help you?"

The owner of the rather high pitched voice was a squat little man of about forty years. He was completely bald and Barnabas couldn't help noticing a serious bowing of his legs as he walked towards him. He sported a typical Jewish nose which seemed low on his face because of a high forehead, which appeared even higher because of his lack of hair. His appearance was far from impressive, but his smile was warm and reassuring, and his eyes were, in stark contrast with the house and the woman who had opened the door, sparkling with life. Barnabas returned the smile and asked if they could be seated, as he was there with an important proposition.

He introduced himself to Saul and explained the purpose of his visit. As he talked, Saul leaned forward, like a man hungry for a meal, but his eyes betrayed a mixture of excitement and concern. He had used his years of isolation wisely, in study of the scriptures and in prayer. Like many before and since, he had been prepared in the school of loneliness for a very public ministry. He was now a broken and humble man, but a man in touch with his Lord. The woman, who opened the door to Barnabas, was his wife, the subject of Saul's prayers across the years and the reason for the look of sadness which now clouded his troubled face. He knew that this was the end. For so long he had prayed and pleaded with her to come to Christ, but she was hostile to any mention of the name of Jesus and scorned the validity of his account of his meeting with Jesus on the highway. Saul knew that he must now decide. He could stay with his wife, or he could leave her in Tarsus and go with his new brother to Antioch. It was not an easy decision to make, although he instantly knew what his choice must be. He loved this stubborn wife of his youth and he would miss her dearly, but he had made a commitment to Christ a long time ago on the road to Damascus and it was clear that he could wait no longer. He took her aside and explained that he was leaving for Antioch. He gave her the option of accompanying him, but she tearfully declined. He took her tenderly in his arms and kissed her eyes and lips, told her that he loved her, and turned and walked away. He took nothing with him and he did not look back. Tears were stinging his eyes and running into his closely cropped beard. He never saw his wife again.

The saints at Antioch welcomed Saul with open arms and hearts. He and Barnabas worked together in perfect harmony, teaching and preaching and pastoring the growing church. It was as though they had known each other for a lifetime. There was no self seeking, just a united desire to serve God and bless the people. Twelve months later they visited Jerusalem together, taking with them some relief supplies, but their reunion with the apostles was sullied with the tragic murder of James the son of Zebedee and the subsequent arrest and incarceration of Peter. They returned to Antioch bearing news of the confusing happenings at Jerusalem and the amazing story of Peter's escape from prison. It was during Peter's extended absence in Rome that the church at Antioch sent Paul and Barnabas on their first missionary journey, leaving Simeon, Lucius, and Manaen to oversee the home church. They visited Cyprus, the birth place of Barnabas, and then journeyed across to Perga in Pamphylia, before heading north as far as Antioch in Pisidia. From there they travelled southeast to Iconium before heading back home to Antioch in Syria. Meanwhile the church at Jerusalem flourished under the leadership of the Lord's brother, James.

The mother church did, of course, implicitly believe in the doctrine of justification by faith in Jesus Christ and in His atoning death on the cross, but unlike Paul and Barnabas, they had not cast off the bondage of old testament law and were still very much tied into the practice of circumcision and other Jewish traditions. When certain visitors went from Jerusalem to visit the Christians in Antioch, they did not hesitate to attempt to force their views on the Syrian church, insisting that they could not possibly belong to the true church, unless they were circumcised. This caused a great deal of resentment amongst the people and both Paul and Barnabas were understandably indignant at this doctrinal intrusion into their work. As a result of the trouble, it was agreed that a group of representatives from Antioch, led by Paul and Barnabas, should visit Jerusalem to try and sort out these very important and divisive issues, before further damage was done to the work of God.

It was into this atmosphere of contention and controversy that Peter was plunged upon his return from Rome. Of course he knew that matters of doctrine needed to be sorted out, but it was also understandable that someone returning from the horrendous scenes that he had witnessed amongst the Jews in Rome, would find this whole saga somewhat petty and incidental. Notwithstanding, he set himself to adjust to his new environment and sought to make whatever contribution he could, in order to help.

It was wonderful to see everyone again, especially his dear friend John, who had left Mary the mother of Jesus in Ephesus, to make the visit back to Jerusalem. It was also good to renew fellowship with Saul, who was now widely known by the name Paul. He had not seen him since before his flight to Rome and there was much catching up to be done. He shared his own experiences and listened with intense interest to Paul's account of his missionary journey.

They both had so much to tell of God's goodness, of lives and communities changed by the power of the Gospel, and of the many miracles which had accompanied the preaching of God's word. They spent almost the whole night, on the day of their reunion, in fellowship and rejoicing and giving glory to God. The following morning it was down to business, as a group of converted Pharisees insisted on debating the matter of circumcision. It was not a pleasant atmosphere and the group of church leaders immediately began arguing and disputing amongst themselves. Peter bowed his head between his knees in an open demonstration of his despair and disgust, that, while souls perished, the men who were responsible for rescuing them engaged in petty debate (vi). Eventually he could contain himself no longer and, rising to his feet, raised his hand for silence.

Peter commanded an authority more powerful than any other single apostle and was a fearless, albeit humble, declarer of truth. The fact was that God had used him to first bring the Gospel to the Gentiles, so if the council at Jerusalem was considering inflicting the Jewish covenant of circumcision upon them, he had a right to make his opinion clear. He began his address by claiming his God given position of authority in the matter and then went on to make his opinion very clear. God was certainly embracing the Gentile world with the Gospel and from Cornelius onwards, thousands were now purified by faith in Jesus Christ and had received the gift of the Holy Ghost. He paused, his heart full of love for the lost, but his eyes ablaze with indignance.

"Why tempt ye God, to put a yoke upon the neck of the disciples, which neither our fathers, nor we, were able to bear?"

His words came from the passionate heart of an evangelist. He paused again, allowing his words to sink into every heart.

"We believe that through the grace of the Lord Jesus Christ we shall be saved, even as they!"

He sat down and the room was stilled with silence. No-one spoke or offered to contradict the apostle. His brother Andrew thought how much Peter had changed since the day he had introduced him to Jesus at Bethabara. The years had moulded steel into his bones and, though he was undoubtedly soft of heart, he was not to be crossed in matters of righteousness. It did seem clear that it was unjust, to say the least, that the non-Jewish Christians at Antioch should be forced to adopt the rite of circumcision, which was not part of their history and had absolutely nothing to do with their relationship with Jesus.

The silence was broken by Barnabas who, with frequent interjections by Paul, gave an account of the many miracles and wonders which they had witnessed God do amongst the Gentiles during their missionary journey. The message undoubtedly was that, if God saw it fitting to pour out His Spirit upon non-Jewish people, it was not for any Jewish Christian in Jerusalem to demand that such people needed in any way to become Jewish. Barnabas and Paul completed their contribution amidst a buzz of conversation. Traditions die hard, especially when rooted in religion and culture, and there were still a number of dissenters who were not convinced.

It took a powerful and diplomatic speech from James, the son of Mary and Joseph, to bring the conference to a satisfactory conclusion. He reminded them of how God sent Peter to Cornelius and that this opening up of the Gospel to the Gentile world was in fact prophesied by the prophet Amos. He concluded that, apart from a few minor exceptions, the Gentile Christians should not be troubled with matters which were a part of Jewish culture. It was further agreed that a delegation be sent from Jerusalem, with Paul and Barnabas, carrying letters from the apostles and elders, reassuring the people that they wished to place no burdens of past traditions upon them. They chose Judas Barsabas and a man called Silas, both of them inspired preachers of the truth, to visit Antioch, deliver the letters and to answer any questions that the people might have.

The delegation carried the message to a gathering of the entire church in Antioch. It was met with great rejoicing and Barsabas and Silas spent several weeks preaching and exhorting the people. Eventually Barsabas returned to Jerusalem, but Silas felt that he should remain in Antioch. It was providential that he did so, for some time afterwards, Paul was to ask him to accompany him on his second missionary journey. Peter, meanwhile, paced Jerusalem, waiting for a new direction for his service. He was not the type to take his ease and was anxious to be about his Father's business. It was not easy for someone who was forever conscious of his commission to preach the Gospel to the world, to discern whether the guidance he felt was from his own spirit, or of the Spirit of God, but his mind was drawn constantly to Antioch. Maybe it was his desire to break free, or perhaps he wanted to work with Paul, but he found himself unable to escape the pull to Syria. He decided to visit Jerusalem's daughter church, to see how he felt when he was there. He could always retrace his steps if nothing transpired and he knew that he was open to God's will.

CHAPTER SIXTEEN

———————

"Oh Holy Christ forgive my sin
When untamed flesh will rise again;
And let Thy fire burn in me
To build Thy church, to honour Thee"

PETER AND JOANNA'S ARRIVAL IN Antioch was met with enthusiastic applause from both leaders and people alike. The presence of the well known fisherman was an encouragement to all and Peter's forthright preaching and evangelistic zeal was a constant inspiration. The people enjoyed listening to his accounts of miracles amongst the downtrodden people in Rome and, as a result, the missionary vision of the church was fanned into a flame. Barnabas and Paul and the other leaders, received him with open arms and within days he felt as though he had been there for years.

Antioch was the third largest city of the Roman Empire with a population of half a million souls. It was founded towards the end of the fourth century BC by one of Alexander the Great's generals, Seleucus Nicator and was named after his father, Antiochus the Great. It stood on the River Orontes at the junction of the trade routes to Damascus, Palestine, Egypt and the Agean. Today it is known as Antakya and is part of Turkey. Peter was impressed with the magnificence of the city, which had the feel of an oriental Rome, although its appearance was that of a Grecian city, embellished by the influence of affluent Rome. It was adorned with intricate statues, theatres, baths and temples, amazing parklands complete with gardens, fountains and cascades. The city was renowned for its obsessive devotion to pleasure, was cosmopolitan in population, and boasted a most awesome temple to Apollo. It was the ideal city to evangelise, because of its importance to the Roman Empire. A powerful church in Antioch was potentially a fountain of evangelism for the whole world. Peter spent days walking the great metropolis and strolling down the broad avenue which dissected the city from east to west. Its four long rows of columns were used to provide covered porticoes on each side of the avenue where the Antiochenes socialised and walked with their families. The avenue stretched for several miles and Peter walked its length like a man sent to claim it as his own.

He was, of course, accustomed to mixing and eating with non Jewish people. His experiences in Rome had established in him the lesson learned through his vision of the sheet and, despite the fact that in Rome he had worked amongst the Jews, he saw no difference between them and Gentiles and was at home in the company of both. He did, in fact, find himself considerably relieved to be free of the Jewish traditions, which were still a source of spiritual encumbrance to the church at Jerusalem. He constantly felt on edge whilst back in Israel, in case he said or did something which cut across Jewish expectations and caused inconvenient controversy. He also enjoyed the food which the people of Antioch enjoyed without fearing that they were transgressing some Kosher law. He began to enjoy the food which had been forbidden to him all his life, food which was not allowed in Israel and not available in the poor districts of Rome.

Everything was wonderful, until a group of Jewish visitors arrived from Judea, the result of an act of friendship on the part of James, and Peter grew nervous in case they objected to his custom of eating with the Gentiles. He began to look over his shoulder and avoid being seen in a non-Jewish setting. Eventually, his fear of man and a desire to please those from whom he desired approval exposed a weakness of character which still lurked in his life, a flaw which could so easily turn him into both a coward and a hypocrite. He distanced himself from his Gentile friends and brothers in Christ and sought the favour of his Judean visitors, by only eating with the Jews. Peter was already a highly respected leader in the church at Antioch and other Jewish Christians followed his example. Even Barnabas took his lead and became party to the schism. All the efforts of the council of Jerusalem and the subsequent letters and assurances were blown away by the very man who was the leading voice in solving the original problem. The shepherd became a stumbling block to the sheep. The man, who had fearlessly obeyed God, became a man pleaser. It was both hypocritical and unacceptable and Paul moved to correct it. A holy indignation rose up in his heart and he purposed to confront Peter publically and expose his hypocrisy. In the presence of a church assembly, he accused Peter of double standards and of undermining the precious doctrine of justification by faith, which he so passionately preached. He told him that he made himself a transgressor, by building again the tradition which he had destroyed and openly called him to repentance.

Peter winced under the correction which came from his friend. His ruddy complexion turned a deeper shade, as his cowardice was exposed before all, but he knew that Paul was right. He was also aware that the wounds of a friend are better than the kisses of an enemy and that his despicable error, which had been such a public matter and had affected the lives of others, should be publically corrected. He sat in silence as Paul's uncompromising judgement fell upon him and waited, head bowed, for a long minute before rising slowly to his feet.

"My brother Paul, fellow ministers of the Gospel, brothers and sisters, I offer no defence for my recent actions. The words of God's servant, Paul, are so obviously correct and my behaviour has been reprehensible. I acted both as a coward and a hypocrite. Regrettably, I also forgot, that I answer to God and to Him alone. I do not need to impress any man and should on all occasions, act honourably and sincerely, before Him alone. I beg your forgiveness. I ask the Gentile Christians here in Antioch to forgive me. I do most certainly believe that there is no difference between you and my fellow Jews and I am sorry for acting otherwise. I ask the forgiveness of our visitors from Judea, for my deceitful actions. I ask forgiveness from my fellow ministers, for the anxiety which I have caused. Most of all I ask the forgiveness of my Lord, who commissioned me to 'feed his sheep' without partiality or favour. May He have mercy upon me and pardon my sin."

He sat down and again silence reigned. Paul wiped a tear from his eye as he stood and crossed the room to his repentant friend. He took Peter by the hand and pulled him to his feet. The two of them embraced in the bonds of Christian love, the tall, strong, burly figure of Peter and the short, stocky, bald-headed Paul, both of them destined to touch the world for the glory of God.

Peter and Joanna stayed at Antioch. The church continued to grow in numbers and in spiritual maturity. It steadied itself and, incited by the Holy Spirit, looked beyond its boundaries, across the empire, to the harvest fields of Europe. It was time for another stirring of the nest. Paul was feeling the pull of the churches which were established on his first missionary journey, the care of which was an abiding burden in his shepherd's heart. He suggested that it was perhaps time to revisit the saints in those cities. Barnabas wanted to take John Mark with them, but Paul was not happy with the way that he had returned home half way through the first expedition and was against his inclusion. A quite serious contention arose between them, the result of which was a parting of the ways. Who knows the mystery of the workings of the Divine mind? Perhaps the orchestration of the dispute came from the Holy Spirit, in order to produce two missionary journeys, instead of one? Whatever, Paul teamed up with Silas and headed for Cilicia, whilst Barnabas and John Mark set sail for Cyprus and there was no acrimony in their parting and, whether divinely planned or not, an attack was launched on two fronts against the kingdom of darkness.

Peter was left as the most experienced leader in the church at Antioch. It was his lot to remain there, with his wife, for the next seven years and in later years he became recognised as the 'first bishop of Antioch'. He laboured much in prayer and in the preaching of the Word and the church grew into a powerful representation of Christ. It was there at Antioch that the followers of Christ were first called 'Christians', a name which signified a church which had finally erased all demarcation lines between Jew and Gentile, uniting both peoples in one covenant with the Father. The church was as ethnically diverse as the city, made up of native Syrians,

Macedonians, Greeks, Romans and Jews, all joined together by the love of Jesus. It worked with passion amongst the teeming thousands of lost souls which thronged the streets of Antioch. Because of its geographical position on the north eastern corner of the Mediterranean Sea, sitting on the coasts of Syria and Asia Minor, it was the city of concourse between Arabia and the West. It became known as the "Gateway to the East". It was Peter's burden to guide the church into becoming such a light in the darkness that it would become, for thousands, the "Gateway to Heaven."

Peter never confined his ministry to the pulpit, although, since his bold address to the crowds on the day of Pentecost, he was a most effective public speaker. He was, however, never more at home than when he was mingling with the people in the streets and the highways, sharing Christ with all and sundry, praying for their sick and offering the hand of mercy and love to the poor. And so a ministry of compassion and caring for the individual became the pattern for the years which Peter spent in Antioch. He laid a foundation of truth and Christ-like living which was to remain solid for many years after his departure.

Chapter Seventeen

―――――――

"When providence would have me move
To cast my nets in other climes,
Direct my barque through waters new:
I'll trim my sail and follow you"

PETER AND JOANNA WERE PERFECTLY content to remain in Antioch for the rest of their lives. It seemed that the needs were endless and the opportunity to build the church and feed the people was an open-ended task. They both felt fulfilled in their work and the expanding church loved and respected them as God's servants. It was all the more disconcerting, therefore, when Peter found his thoughts involuntarily turning to Rome. It seemed as though, whenever he went aside to pray, pictures of Rome played upon his mind. He began to dream about the city, that he was walking by the banks of the River Tiber, looking back at the impressive stone buildings which stood like symbolic warnings of ever expanding world domination. Invariably he heard the voice of God in his dreams, like distant thunder rolling across the heavens, always saying the same thing, "You are Peter, and upon this rock I will build my church and the gates of hell will not prevail against it." His imagination gazed into the fast moving currents of the Tiber and spoke into its grey, swirling waters, "But I have no power to stand against the majesty of Rome. It encompasses the world with its violence and all men are subdued by its dominance. I am just a fisherman, fishing for a few souls, that I might rescue them from their own fallen natures." But back came the reply, and the thunder was much closer now, "But Peter, did I not show you precisely where to cast your nets, when your efforts had borne no fruit in your nights upon the Galilee, and did not my direction give you fish, in number, beyond your dreams? Fish for men in the sea of Rome and I will multiply the harvest and gather it from the outer regions of the world." Suddenly Peter seemed as though he was lifted up, above the city, rising higher, until he looked down upon the world and he could see the Roman legions spreading out across the earth, like the waters cover the sea and they were plundering and killing and subduing the tribes of the earth. Then, it was as though he zoomed in upon the great tide of marching men and saw their weapons of war and the sun glinting on their swords, but then he noticed that some of them were not carrying swords, but fishing nets upon their shoulders, and he knew that they were nets for catching men. Then the voice of God was there again, this time speaking gently as Peter rose like a bird into the clear heavens, "Fish in Rome, my son, and the Romans that you catch, will fish around the world."

Peter asked Joanna and the leadership of the church to pray with him concerning the call to Rome that was upon his heart. He did not know what to do. His dilemma was made more acute because of his own desire to remain in Antioch and he knew very well that human inclinations often masquerade as the voice of God. He sincerely desired the mind of God's Spirit and was not confident in his own discernment. After several weeks of prayerful contemplations the interested parties found a place of unanimous witness that it did seem good to the Holy Ghost that Peter and his wife set out for Rome. Arrangements were made and fond and tearful farewells took place. In the July of 57 AD, they boarded ship for Corinth on the first leg of their journey to Italy.

It was a hot day, but they set sail against a moderate westerly breeze which obligingly lifted a light spray to cool the deck. Peter loved it! This was his home, second only to the will of God, but when the two combined and his spirit united with the Divine Spirit on the open sea, Peter was in the seventh heaven. The sun, the wind, the spray, the pitching of the boat and the foam left in its wake, all were like medicine to the aging man from Galilee. Joanna was not so sure. This was the first time in her life that she had ventured onto the Great Sea and her constitution was not as acclimatised to her new environment, as was her husband's. Knowledge that they were both following the leading of the Comforter, however, was her strength and she hummed a Jewish love song as she gripped the side of the ship's bow.

Corinth sat at the western side of the isthmus which formed a four mile wide land bridge between the southern landmass and central Greece. The city controlled harbours on each side of the isthmus, one receiving shipping from the Aegean Sea to the east and the other from the Ionian Sea to the west. The city of two seas therefore commanded the trade routes between Asia and Rome. Crews of small ships actually dragged their boats across a paved road, which ran across the isthmus, to re-launch them on the other side, to save a sea journey of more than two hundred miles. Larger ships unloaded cargo and carried it across the divide, to reload it onto other ships. Across the centuries, various plans were made to cut a canal across the land bridge.

Alexander the Great, Julius Caesar, and Caligula, all gave serious consideration to the project. The future emperor, Nero, actually held a ceremony for the commencement of the work, using Jewish slaves for labour, but the scheme was subsequently abandoned. The Canal was finally built by the French at the end of the nineteenth century.

The atmosphere in Corinth was pleasant, not because it was pure, but because it was without restraint. A feeling of freedom filled the air, but it was a freedom to do evil, which, beneath the silk surface and the deceiving music, ate away at the moral fabric of society. The city was teeming with Greeks, Jews and Romans and innumerable other ethnic groups. Commerce from around the world poured wealth into the community and with it, the licence to party. The multicultural society was splashed across its huge market place and the beauty of the city was crowned with the ruins of the famous temple of Aphrodite, the goddess of love, which proudly stood on the hill of the Acropolis. Dozens of wine shops catered to the thousands of sailors and tradesmen who passed through from all over the world and the one thousand priestesses of Aphrodite, an ever present reminder of the faded glory of the temple, acted the part of sacred prostitutes and lured the men into their webs of vice. They descended from the Acropolis every night, to ply their trade amongst the unsuspecting and the foolish, and Corinth degenerated into a monolith of drunkenness, debauchery and unspeakable filth. The abundance of orgies, held in the name of the Paphian goddess, became as notorious as those of Asherah. Moral standards were at zero and the culture of lust unfortunately infiltrated the fledgling church, which was founded by Paul after his visit to Athens in 51 AD. He had found there a man by the name of Aquila and his wife Priscilla, Christian Jews who were evicted from Rome when Claudius made his edict. They were tentmakers, a skill which Paul shared with them, and they worked together in preaching the Gospel in the Jewish synagogue as well as to the Greeks. This was the beginning of the Corinthian church.

Peter never intended staying for long in Corinth. He did, in fact, only purpose a two or three day layover before continuing with his journey, but he took time to visit the Christians there and they asked him to do some preaching and teaching amongst them. He was nervous about interfering in a work which was birthed by Paul and sought to keep his teaching simple and to the point. The last thing he wanted to do was to undermine the work which Paul had already done. Several times he heard mention of Aquila and Priscilla, who had accompanied Paul when he left Corinth to go on to Ephesus. Evidently Aquila was a native of a city called Sinope, capital of the province of Pontus on the south coast of the Black Sea.

Comparatively speaking, the church in Corinth was upholding a standard of righteousness in an otherwise carnal and depraved society, but he was troubled about the immaturity of many of the people and was particularly concerned that the church should maintain the standards of Christian purity in the midst of the wickedness of Corinth. Although the power of the Holy Spirit was evident amongst them, he strongly suspected that a number of the people were living in fornication and there were even rumours that one man in the church was sleeping with his step-mother. He stayed for two months altogether and the people enjoyed his charismatic and forthright approach. When the time came, however, he was more than a little relieved to move on. He prayed that God would give Paul wisdom in his handling of this fragile group. He learned sometime later that, after his departure, the people were arguing amongst themselves who the best leader was, Paul, Peter, Apollos or Jesus. Part of him wished that he had never gone, but at least he could pray and he had every confidence that Paul would address the problems as he saw fit.

On the day of his departure from Corinth, Peter and Joanna left their lodgings in the city and set out for the harbour on the Ionian Sea side of the Isthmus, intending to board a ship that would take them westwards, through the Corinthian Gulf and the Straits of Patra and onwards to Italy. They had been walking for about ten minutes when Peter's pace slowed and a troubled expression clouded his normally bright face. Joanna looked at him with concern.

"Peter, is something wrong? You don't look very good."

Peter stopped and faced his wife. He assured her that there was nothing wrong, except that he felt as though they were walking in the wrong direction.

"Something doesn't feel right," he said. "I keep feeling that we should be going east, not west. Do you remember the people we heard about who went with Paul, the man called Aquila? Somebody said that he came from a place called Sinope in Asia Minor. Well, that name Sinope has been in my mind since yesterday and, while we have been walking, it is filling my whole mind. I think God wants us to take a ship to Sinope."

"But I thought that we were supposed to be going to Rome, Peter. I don't understand."

Peter paused and then spoke in a tone that showed that his mind was made up.

"We will go to Rome Joanna, but the time is not right! I believe that it is right for us to turn round and take a ship for Sinope."

Sinope was a flourishing Greek port in the centre of the south coast of the Black Sea in the area known as Pontus (now a part of modern Turkey). Under Roman rule it became the most important port on the Black Sea and so the maritime traffic was abundant and frequent. It was not difficult for Peter and Joanna to find passage. They carried their bags to the Aegean side of the Isthmus and boarded a merchant ship bound for Pontus. The following morning they were skimming through the calm waters by Athens, then northwards through the Aegean. They passed without incident through the Dardanelles, across the Sea of Marmara, then through the Bosporus Straits at Byzantium and into the Black Sea. Hugging the northern coastline of Asia Minor they then sailed eastwards and six days later came to Sinope.

The province of Pontus had a mountainous terrain, desolate and barren in the east but lush and fertile in the west. The mountains of the east were rich in iron ore, whilst the west produced wine, grain, honey, wax and wood, as well as cherries, which were first taken to Europe from Pontus. Peter once more experienced the excitement of destiny as his feet touched terra firma. He was confident that this was the place to which the Holy Spirit had brought him. Here, another cell of the universal church of Jesus Christ would be born.

It was virgin territory, but Peter preached with great boldness under the anointing of the Holy Spirit. He debated with all and sundry, in market squares and lodging houses and places of religion, pointing them to Jesus and showing Him to be the Saviour of the world. Everywhere this man went he was driven with a passion to win the lost, by preaching Christ crucified. He prayed for the sick and commanded healing in the name of Jesus and many were set free from numerous types of sicknesses. He visited a local tentmaker who, in his youth, was acquainted with Aquila and, through him, he managed to contact Aquila's family and had the joy of leading them to faith in Christ. Joanna ministered to the women and told them stories of the miracles which she had seen Jesus do and explained to them the meaning of the cross. Within six months the nucleus of a church was established and people were being added to it on a regular basis. Then Peter began to feel restless. He stood alone on a cold January morning, gazing out across the sea. The mountains to the east were blanketed with snow and a biting wind was blowing in across the water from the north. The sky was a seamless blanket of grey cloud. He suddenly felt alone and lost and insignificant before the huge challenge that was the need of the world. He knew that it was time to move on, but he had no idea which way to go.

CHAPTER EIGHTEEN

"Blest be the bond that does not break,

Forever linking souls in loves deep tie;

When last farewells on earth are said,

They only last 'til death is dead"

AFTER MUCH PONDERING AND PRAYER, Peter and Joanna moved east to Amisus and then followed the River Iris southwards to Amaseia (modern Amasya), a city seated in the centre of a region of fertile plains and magnificently situated in a narrow gorge at the southern edge of the Pontus mountains. The only exit from Pontus to the south was through one of these river valleys. The rugged mountains stood like huge sentinels, towering above the tight mountain ravine, their snow capped peaks glittering white against the azure blue of the sky. Peter was fascinated with the sheer rock cliffs which drew his eyes upwards and he marvelled at the majestic eagle which hovered motionless above the canyon. He could only imagine what this place would be like in the summer months when the fragrance of sweet smelling flowers would be carried on the breeze through this most exotic and fortunate of towns. He felt like an explorer who had ingeniously exposed the hidden, secret beauty of a previously undiscovered paradise. He stood and wrapped his arms around his beloved Joanna and breathed in the cold, clean, winter air.

They followed the river south eastwards until they came to Tokat in Cappadocia, a small town which sat comfortably at the foot of a huge jagged rock. He announced the Gospel message to the people. From here they turned to the west into the province of Galatia. Peter was aware that Paul had already visited the region and, although he wanted to be a blessing to the Christian communities that existed as a result, he looked for virgin territory, where he could perhaps enlighten the Jewish populations in the things concerning Christ Jesus. Much of Paul's preaching centred around Antioch in Pisidia, so Peter went further north to Ancyra, a community which became the capital town of the Roman province of Galatia in BC 25. Paul never travelled this far north in Galatia, but in the purposes of God, Peter and Joanna preached Christ crucified to the population of Greeks, Jews, Romans and Gauls. Wherever he could, he sought out his Jewish countrymen and unfolded the truth to them concerning Jesus, using their own Jewish Torah as the vehicle of revelation. Many people believed. Everywhere Peter went he boldly announced Christ as Saviour and healer, and many signs and wonders were done in the name of Jesus.

Peter was intrigued by the spectacular Augusteum Temple which was erected in honour of Rome and its first emperor, Caesar Augustus. Its white marble walls reflected the rays of the morning sun and turned it into a glittering jewel of light against its rocky backdrop. His mind entertained the fantasy of erecting such an edifice in honour of his Lord, but knowing such a notion defied reason he rested on the fact that the glory of Jesus was to be seen in changed lives and in the body which is His church. Little did he know that the church that was now being born in Ancyra through his ministry was destined to grow into a powerful force for righteousness and would one day occupy that same marble temple, which he so much admired.

Again Peter felt it was time to move on, this time north westwards into Bithynia, a province which was closely allied to Pontus to the east, the place where Peter's circle of ministry had begun. This was the place which the Holy Spirit did not allow Paul to enter, calling him rather to set sail westwards from Mysia, across the Aegean Sea, to Macedonia and Philippi. Now Peter enters the harvest field that God had reserved for him, with the responsibility of that calling weighing heavily upon his shoulders. He arrived at the city of Nicea, a rectangular shaped walled town positioned at the edge of a lake of the same name. It was dissected by two major roads in the shape of a cross, one running north to south, the other, east to west. The city had four gates which could all be seen from a raised plinth in the town centre. Here the fisher of men once more cast his net and the souls of men and women were stirred by the truth. He always preached with passion and urgency, often weeping as he pleaded for the people to yield to the overtures of Divine mercy. Many believed and were baptised into the Father, Son and Holy Ghost. Peter taught them to pray and preach the Gospel to others. He encouraged and inspired them to take up the baton and do the work of an evangelist. The church grew and prospered as God confirmed His word with miracles.

When Peter and Joanna finally took leave of the Christians in Nicea several months later and headed south into Asia, he paused on the plain and looked back at the grey stone walls of the city. He felt a love for this place and the new born Christians he had left to pray for her. He gripped Joanna's hand and a lump rose in his throat.

"I feel something special about this place," he said.

He was right. The church grew and prospered under the anointing of the Holy Spirit and long after Peter was dead, a grand cathedral was constructed in Nicea, named the Cathedral of St Sophie and it was here in the year AD 325 that Christian bishops came together from around the world, at the invitation of Emperor Constantine, and put together the statement of fundamental beliefs which is still known as the Nicene Creed to this day, observed by Christian churches all over the world (vii).

From Nicea the apostle headed south, skirting the eastern coast of the lake, and journeyed towards Prusa on the north western slopes of Mount Uludag. Here he enjoyed a blessed reunion with his natural brother Andrew, who was actively preaching the Gospel in the city. It was here that Andrew was eventually martyred and a church was built which bears his name.

From Prusa (modern day Bursa) Peter and Joanna continued their journey south. They had their sights set on Ephesus, where the Apostle John lived with Mary the mother of Jesus. Peter had not seen Mary since his escape from prison and subsequent flight from Jerusalem. His belly churned with excitement at the thought of meeting her again. They passed through Pergamum and Izmir and, after several weeks of travel and not a little preaching of the Gospel en route, the huge city of Ephesus, with its 250,000 inhabitants, lay before them. Peter could feel the wickedness of this massive metropolis of paganism and his spiritual senses recoiled at the stench of immorality and idol worship that this city, with its dominating temple to the goddess Diana, portrayed. He also discerned the battle that raged in the heavens for control of this most strategic place. His spiritual eyes saw beyond the light covering of cloud which veiled the firmament beyond, to where demonic forces vainly sought to resist the angelic hosts which moved against them with the banner of the cross. A thrill of excitement coursed through his veins and his flesh tingled in response to the words which spilled from his lips.

"This citadel of darkness and evil will become the domain of the Holy Ghost. The people of Ephesus will become worshippers of the One True God, and, from this city, the world will be touched by the saving power of Jesus Christ."

He turned and took Joanna's hand in his own. Tears were flowing down her face. She knew that her husband's words were prophetic. This was one of those special moments when God makes a declaration that no man or devil can gainsay. This city, which was presently the centre of Roman government, was destined to become a seat of world evangelism.

They entered the city from the north, passing the city stadium (Hippodrome) on their left. This was the place where gladiators fought to the death with wild animals and was accessed through an impressive monumental gate. They did not pause to investigate. Peter was anxious to begin the search for his friends.

Everywhere, there was evidence of affluence and indulgence. The city was obviously a centre of art and leisure, where music and theatre and costume were of great importance. They entered the city proper and came to the eastern end of the central avenue known as Harbour Street. Peter stood with his back to the avenue and gazed with awe at the 24,000 seat open-air amphitheatre. He turned and protectively holding his wife's arm, began a tentative walk down Harbour Street towards the port. The street was a full 36 feet wide and adorned with marble slabs and Colonnades. Shops and galleries lined the road on either side, many of them sporting impressive arches, and people from every part of the world thronged the avenue. Romans and Greeks and Jews mingled with flower girls and street vendors. Military commands unified with the yells of slave drivers and the menacing sounds of cracking whips. Already they could see the proud temple of Diana rising 130 feet into the air, standing as though gazing out to sea, a challenge to all who dare enter its domain. They came to the Harbour Baths, another breathtaking structure and one of the largest buildings in Ephesus, no less than 160m wide, 170m long and 28m high. Then the harbour itself opened up before them, a colourful and noisy display of ships and boats, military, commercial and domestic from around the world. It seemed as though the harbour and the sheer number of souls which moved like slow moving ants around its edges emphasised the impossible task of trying to find two people in a city of one quarter of a million.

Peter lifted his heart to the One who had called him one night to walk on water, once told him to fish for a coin to pay their taxes, the One who miraculously sent an angel to break him out of prison. He needed help now to find John and Mary.

"This way Peter!"

Joanna pulled gently at his sleeve and led him down to the harbour's edge. Boats were moored tightly along the wall, gently nudging each other in time with the rise and fall of the water, and people embarked and disembarked as businessmen plied their respective trades. A fishing boat was unloading its catch into wooded crates and passersby were purchasing fresh fish for their evening meal. Joanna pulled him closer to the scene.

"This way Peter, I feel we should go this way!"

"No, no my friend, you ask far too much. I am not ignorant of the value of your wares. I will give you five dupondius and no more!"

Peter jerked to a halt. He would recognise that voice anywhere in the world. His eyes darted to the man at the front of the queue for fish. He had his back to him. He was of stocky build and his greying hair was thinning on top, but Peter was acquainted with the way this man stood, the familiar bending of his left knee as he stood and the tilt of his shoulder to the left.

"John!" he yelled. "John, over here, look who has come to see you!"

Within seconds the old friends were wrapped in each other's arms. Joanna wept with joy as she saw the two fishermen from Galilee, laughing and weeping and laughing again on each other's shoulders. They stood back and each gazed into the other's ageing face, and then they were embracing again, squeezing the breath from their lungs.

"How did you find me?" John asked. "How did you know that I was here?"

"We just walked through the town and came to the harbour and I prayed the Lord would help us and Joanna felt that we should come this way. It must have been the Lord John; remember how He told us where to go and find the ass when He was going to ride into Jerusalem? He knew exactly where it was and He knew where you were. How's Mary? Is she still alive?"

"She is indeed, my friend. I will take you to her, but wait." He called across to the fish seller, "Hey, I'll take those fish and as many again. Nine dupondius, ok?"

His reunion with Mary was amazing. John walked Peter and Joanna beyond the city limits and up into the surrounding hills. They eventually came to a clearing on a grassy shelf overlooking a tree strewn valley which had drawn the sea into the shelter of a large cove. There, in the most picturesque and tranquil setting that Peter had ever experienced, John had built the mother of the Christ a beautiful little stone house, where she could end her troubled life in peace. She was now seventy nine years old and her skin was wrinkled and her face lined with the scars of age. Her eyes, however, shone with the light of an inner spirit, which still sparkled with the dew of youth.

For the briefest of moments the perplexed look of non-recognition furrowed her brow and then she screamed with joy as she threw herself into the arms of her old friend. When she eventually extracted herself from his embrace, her face was bathed with the tears of joy and it was as though a dozen years were lifted from her account. She greeted

Joanna with similar enthusiasm, before tugging gently on her arm in order to subject her to a tour of her tiny home. The following hours were filled with a mixture of laughter and tears, memories and stories from the carpenters shop in Nazareth to the amazing tours of Galilee with Jesus. She wanted to talk about her beloved son James, bishop of the Jerusalem church, who was martyred just a year before at the command of Ananus, high priest in Jerusalem. Not only had she lost her son, but she felt that the last tie with her beloved Joseph was now broken. For a while after the news reached her in the June of 62 AD she prayed that the Lord would take her home. She had no longer been able to see any real purpose in her life. Peter was understanding of her loss and made her laugh with anecdotes from the life of her son, who had been so particular about every detail of righteous living that he earned himself the title of "James the Just".

They talked long into the night about the work of making disciples of all nations and Peter told her about his six year diversion on the road to Rome and the fruit which had been borne in the lives of many people and places across Asia Minor. At the mention of Rome, Mary appeared troubled.

"Things are not good in Rome, Peter. I feel deeply concerned about the church there. I feel that this emperor Nero is a very wicked young man and a great enemy of God's people. Sometimes, when I close my eyes to sleep, I see much blood. Heavy clouds of oppression lower over the city and in the distance I hear the screams, blood curdling screams, of those who love my Son. Dark wings of demonic powers seem to carry the torments of hell to the innocent and undeserving. Many times I have awakened from my sleep, sobbing because of the sorrows of the afflicted. I fear great trouble for the future, for the inhabitants of Rome. Be careful Peter, for if the Holy Spirit has commissioned you to go to Rome, you must remember all the lessons that you have learned in former years, whether by example, teaching, or through personal failure."

She leaned forward in her chair and touched his hand softly with her finger tips. He saw the combined agony of love and care, tearing at her eyes. He knelt at her side.

"I will go where the Master leads me Mary. He will not fail us. Please do not worry; I feel no fear, for we are in His hands."

He kissed her cheek and then turned the conversation to more joyful matters.

Peter and Joanna remained in Ephesus for several months. They enjoyed edifying times in fellowship with Timothy, a convert of the apostle Paul and now leader of the church in the city. Peter stood daily on the steps of the city library, accosting Jewish intellectuals and persuading them concerning Jesus of Nazareth from the writings of the Torah. He also visited other churches in the area, ministering to the saints as he felt led. Smyrna to the north and Sardis to the north east were his favourites, especially the latter, because it housed a huge Jewish population, an ideal and fruitful fishing ground for one who was particularly burdened for people from his own ethnic roots. It was a new city of some 120,000 souls, rebuilt by Emperor Tiberius after a devastating earthquake destroyed the old city in 17 AD. John and Paul had already done considerable evangelism in the city and a sizable group of Christians met to worship God. They needed Peter's encouragement. The atmosphere of Sardis was one of deep spiritual apathy and the Christians were inclined to dearth.

Peter stirred them up with passionate exhortations to right living in the power and life of the Holy Spirit and reminded them of their responsibility to preach the Gospel.

It was a wonderful time of service and fellowship. Happy evenings on the slope outside Mary's mountain home, watching the sun sliding into the Aegean Sea in a blaze of golden glory while they talked of the Kingdom and the second advent of the Saviour, were some of the most sweet and peaceful times of their whole lives. There were moments when the presence of Jesus covered that sacred place and they wept tears of joy as they held hands and sang of the wonder of God's love. Then came the morning that Peter woke from his sleep and the voice of the Spirit spoke clearly to his mind.

"Now is the time Peter! It is time for you to go to Rome. Storm clouds are gathering and my people need you. The harvest is great and the labourers are few."

The winds of change were blowing across the lives of these committed ones and adjustments had to be made. John would not always be in Ephesus. Dark times were ahead for the son of thunder, times that would take him as a prisoner to Rome and then into exile on the Island of Patmos. Here he was destined to receive the revelation of Jesus Christ and visions of the end times, which would produce the content of the last book in the New Testament. Timothy and the churches in the area must learn to operate without these foundation apostles and trust God directly for their future guidance. John would return to spend his last days in Ephesus, but Peter was about to leave, never to return.

It was a sad and emotional farewell. Peter knew that he would never see Mary again on this earth and something told him that the same applied to John. Mary did not accompany them to the harbour, but John stood waving half-heartedly, as the faithful couple boarded their ship for Rome.

"Cast your nets on the right side, Peter," he called to his fisherman friend and Peter smiled as he remembered the 153 fish they had caught that morning on Lake Galilee as Jesus issued a similar command. That was the memorable morning Jesus asked him if he loved Him. Then He said, "Feed My sheep." It was on that same occasion that Jesus told him that he would eventually lay down his life for His Lord. Peter had a strange feeling that in Rome, he would do both.

CHAPTER NINETEEN

"What unrelenting pain is this,
Which tears the body of our Lord?
Can persecution be denied,
And evil, still be turned aside?"

ON THE 15TH DECEMBER AD 37 in Antium, just before dawn, nine months after the death of the emperor Tiberius, the beautiful Agrippina, daughter of Germanicus, gave birth to a baby son and named him Lucius Domitius Ahenobarbus. He was the son of Cnaeus Domitius Ahenobarbus, a man of distinguished Roman ancestry. When Lucius reached the age of two years Caligula exiled his mother to the Pontian Islands and when his father died shortly afterwards, his inheritance was confiscated. In 49 AD, with her uncle Claudius now emperor of Rome, Agrippina returned to Rome, married Claudius and the following year, Lucius became the adopted son of the emperor and was henceforth known as Nero. He was married to Claudius' daughter Octavia and in 51 AD was named by Claudius as his heir-apparent.

In the year 54 AD Agrippina, driven by personal lust for power and ambitious for her teenage son, murdered her husband by poisoning him and Nero came to power, with his domineering and bad tempered mother acting as regent. Although barely seventeen years old, he soon made it clear that he considered himself to be the supreme head of Rome and had his mother housed in a separate residence, away from the corridors of power. Considering his brother Britannicus a threat to his position, he strengthened his hold on power, by poisoning him at a dinner party, which he held at his palace on the 11th February 55 AD.

Nero has polluted the pages of history with his debauched life. He was bored with politics and the affairs of state. He preferred to spend his time indulging in the satisfying of his senses. His vices were extravagant and plumbed the depths of depravity. His indescribable wickedness was equalled only by his conceit. He was a handsome, but seriously freckled youth, with dark blond hair and glassy grey-blue eyes. He had a thick neck, a protuberant belly and skinny legs. His vanity knew no bounds and he sought sexual conquests amongst male and female alike. It is said that he even slept with his own brother Britannicus shortly before the fatal dinner party in 55 AD. He was greedy, cruel and given to gluttony. He organised dinners which sometimes lasted for more than twelve hours and were accompanied by filthy and obscene behaviour, which turned them into orgies of unparalleled licentiousness. He considered himself beyond the law. He was blind to any standards of human decency and became the willing slave of his own perversions.

In 58 AD Nero began an affair with Poppaea Sabina, the very beautiful wife of his friend, Marcus Salvius Otho. When his mother voiced her opposition and sided with Nero's wife Octavia, he made several unsuccessful attempts on her life, before finally succeeding when he instructed an assassin to beat and stab her to death. He then visited the scene and laughingly washed his hands in her blood. He later arranged for Octavia to be executed, ironically on a false charge of adultery, so that he could marry his mistress. She was only nineteen years of age at the time of her death. It was not, however, a lasting triumph for Poppaea, for four years later Nero kicked her to death in a fit of temper, while she was pregnant with his child. Rarely has time produced a man so universally base, the very embodiment of evil, and the antithesis of Christian culture.

He spent his energies in the promotion of art and theatre, even doing the unthinkable and actually performing himself as an actor on stage. He organised music competitions, thought himself something of a poet and singer, and gloried in spectacular sporting events, arranging chariot races and athletic tournaments. His gigantic ego, coupled with absolute world power, gradually evolved into madness. He became dangerous in the extreme.

Peter and Joanna approached Rome from the south on the highway known as the Appian Way. The scene had not changed from how he remembered it fifteen years before. Poor people walking, the somewhat better off riding on mules or donkeys, those of higher social standing were on horseback, or in some form of carriage, or were being carried on litters by numerous slaves. The very rich idly reclined in more luxuriously decorated coaches, complete with curtains and cushions and often proceeded by a pair of uniformed outriders. Pedlars with their back-packs jostled with merchants and their carrying slaves, peasants and layabouts stood back to allow passage to a regiment of soldiers, or a squadron of Roman cavalry resplendent in their fine uniforms. It was a noisy, moving sea of humanity, waiting for the evangelist to once more lift his voice in their midst.

The year was 63 AD and although Nero had been in power for nine years and his excesses were well known, the general populous of Rome were not discontent. Because Rome was the capital of the empire, with a population of two million souls, it was important that the thousands of poor people in addition to the unemployed were kept reasonably happy. Insurrection was an anathema. It was therefore ensured that, although many were living in quite desperate circumstances, none were actually starving. The names of 200,000 citizens were on a list to receive a monthly allowance of corn, paid for from the coffers of the imperial treasury. Whatever, as Peter entered the city, he was amazed at the sheer number of beggars, who crouched like lost animals in the gutters, each one a precious soul for whom the Saviour died. Rome was like any major city of the twenty first century; it contained the very poor and the very rich and a mass of hard working people from doctors to painters and sculptors to masons, in between. The architecture ranged from the spectacular palaces on the Palatine Hill and the splendour of the Circus Maximus stadium, to the hovels of the slums on the banks of the Tiber. This was the place of Peter's final assignment, as it had been his first.

Christianity in Rome was on the increase. At the time of Peter's arrival there were several thousand Christians meeting, many of them in secret, in various small groups across the city. They were made up of Jews, Greeks, freed slaves and Romans of a higher social background. Peter was surprised that he was not only remembered from his first visit to Transtiberim, but was actually honoured amongst the people as their first bishop. It seemed that his ministry had laid a foundation which others had built upon and, although despised and opposed for its monotheist doctrine, the church seemed poised for growth. Peter and Joanna enthusiastically went from house to house, encouraging the people to walk closely with the Lord. Peter preached the gospel with great boldness and many miracles of healing were done and many souls were added to the Kingdom. Songs of praise often rolled down streets where poor benighted men and women sat in great darkness and, touched by the music of souls set free, came to receive Christ as Saviour and Lord.

Peter felt a sense of urgency pulling at his spirit, not only to win the lost, but to establish these people in a deep walk with God. An aura of disquiet touched his heart, a foreboding for the future, and the apprehension that Mary had expressed for the future of Rome was forever in his mind. If storms of persecution were gathering on the horizon for these sheep, then it was his Christ-given duty to feed them. Never has a man risen more to his task of shepherding God's people as this aging fisherman now rose up to lead the saints. He showed strength of character, a commitment and devotion to duty, which was an example to them all. He laughed with them and he wept with them. He taught them the sayings of Christ and he showed them how to pray. He led them to trust God, until the reality of His presence was the key to all their lives. He urged them to live, and move, and have their being, in Christ. He moved from place to place with untiring energy. Sometimes Joanna pleaded with him to rest, but he seemed driven to go on, as though the sun was setting and his time of opportunity was brief. She often found him weeping, sobbing for the people, and when she asked him why, he said he did not know. In addition to all this, he took to sitting up in the night, listening to the voice of the

Holy Spirit and writing letters to the Christians in the places where he had preached the gospel throughout his travels. She glanced at the tear stained pages one morning and found that he had written, "To the strangers scattered throughout Pontus, Galatia, Cappadocia, Asia and Bithinia." He had not forgotten them. He had moved on as God directed him, but he carried the love and the burden of the church with him wherever he went. His premonition of approaching persecution was evident in his writing. Convinced that any persecution of the church in Rome would spread throughout the empire, he warned God's people of the possibility of manifold trials and the distress and heaviness which they would produce, but also pointed out that God would use such tribulation in their lives, to produce deeper faith, tried and perfected in the flames, until pure as gold.

On the night of July 19th 64 AD the cry went out that Rome was burning. A blazing inferno was consuming the shops which lined the Circus Maximus. Peter ran with thousands of other citizens to help fight the fire, but gangs of ruffians barred their way. The fire raged out of control, fanned by strong winds, tearing through the narrow streets. It was hopeless. It devoured the buildings like a hungry beast. For six days the fire consumed all in its path, before it was finally brought under control. Then it reignited and burned for a further three days. Ten out of Romes' fourteen districts were destroyed. The 800 yr old temple of Jupiter Stator and the Atrium Vestae, hearth of the Vestal Virgins, were lost. Two thirds of Rome was wiped from the map. Rumour spread as fast as the fire, that Nero himself was the instigator of the destruction, driven by a passion to rebuild the city after his own design and to bear his name, Neropolis. The Roman historian, Tacticus, just a young teenager at the time of the fire, claims that Nero calmly watched Rome burn whilst playing his music with frivolous contempt, in the tower of Maecenas. Thousands perished in the holocaust of flames and thousands more lost their homes and businesses. The people were confused and angry. It was widely believed that Nero was guilty, but fear quenched open rebellion.

As public opinion turned against the emperor he became anxious for his safety and position. He needed a scapegoat to bear the burden of guilt and thereby save his own skin. He resolved to serve the responsibility for the fire onto the Christian community. He hated the Christians and the man called Peter, who was motivating them to proselytise and persuade people to worship their God rather than Nero and the gods of Rome. He saw his opportunity to escape the consequences of his despicable crime and at the same time deal a vicious blow against the sect of the Christians. He openly accused the Christian church of subversion against the authority of Rome and of firing the city. And so began one of the worst persecutions levelled against Christians in the history of humankind.

Nero's cruelty was unleashed with a frightening lack of restraint. He occupied himself in the devising of all manner of atrocious and barbaric acts against the followers of Christ. His soldiers rounded up groups of Christians and stitched them into the skins of animals, before feeding them to wild dogs, which savaged them and tore them to death. He took delight in tearing men from their wives and having them publically crucified on the sides of the main road into the city. Children were torn from their mother's arms and forced to watch as they were brutally raped and murdered. Many were dipped in wax before being suspended on poles in Nero's gardens. They were then burned alive, while the evil emperor enjoyed the spectacle of his flower beds illuminated with human torches. His abandonment to unspeakable cruelty and unrestrained evil was so wanton, that it did little to alleviate his lack of popularity before the people. Even the stomachs of hardened Romans found such indiscriminate killing of the innocent, too much to digest.

If Peter's time in Ephesus was his most joyous, his latest appointment was his most difficult. His experience, his pastoral care and leadership, were essential to this suffering church of Jesus Christ. Peter now realised why the Lord had sent him to Rome and why this time was so right. He laboured long and hard, seeking to protect and encourage the people. He ministered comfort to the bereaved, always talking to them of the eternal world of everlasting peace, a place where sorrow and weeping were no more, where their slaughtered loved ones were at rest in the presence of the Saviour. He was always strong before the people, but privately he wailed in deepest anguish for the suffering they endured, calling out to God to somehow intervene and stop this dreadful holocaust. Sometimes it seemed as though Nero grew bored of his bloody pastime and the ferocity of the persecution appeared to subside. Amazingly, however, and undeniably, despite the murder of so many, the Christians seemed to multiply. The love of Jesus and the power of the Gospel were more effective than the forces of evil that opposed them, and the church continued to grow. So once more the tide of hatred rose to consume and destroy and wave after wave of violence wrought havoc amongst the peace loving Christians of Rome.

In the summer of 66 AD, back in Jerusalem, Eleazar, son of the high priest, persuaded the temple authorities to cease offering the daily sacrifice as a prayer for the protection of the Roman emperor. This action, in first century Palestine, was regarded as a serious insult to Nero and was tantamount to a declaration of revolutionary intent against the authority of Rome. From that point, war between the Romans and the Jews was inevitable. It eventually became reality and culminated in the destruction of Jerusalem in 70 AD. Meanwhile, the noises of revolution in Judea served to distract Nero from his persecution of the Christians in Rome and the hostilities ceased. He appointed Vespasian, recently returned from campaigning in Britain, to go to Palestine and subdue the revolt, whilst he, with typical disregard for responsibility, but to the relief of thousands, embarked upon a tour of Greece. He was gone throughout the whole of 67 AD, entering artistic and athletic competitions and revelling in the awards and prizes which were undeservedly showered upon him.

Peter and Joanna used the time of respite for the consolidation of the church, combining pastoral care with a new surge of evangelistic outreach in the city. The apostle Paul, who by this time was incarcerated in the prisoner quarters of Nero's Praetorian Guard, passionately preached the Gospel and won converts, even amongst the soldiers who were chained to him, so bringing the church within the precincts of Caesar's palace. It seemed as though God poured out His blessings as a recompense for the manifold sufferings of the people and miracles and many signs and wonders were done amongst the poor and needy. Peter went from house to house and group to group, pouring out the love of Christ, praying for the people and encouraging young and old in the ways of the Lord. His energy knew no bounds. He was as full of the Holy Ghost, as he was on that amazing day years before in the upper room in Jerusalem.

The peace of the church was shattered at the end of 67 AD when Nero, his ego yet more inflated by the false flatteries which he attracted on his travels, rode into Rome and immediately took up his war against the followers of Christ. The obvious energy of the Christian community poured fuel onto his hatred and it boiled over into a passionate campaign to extinguish the light of Christ. The pillaging, rape and murder began all over again. Nero seemed determined to fill his cup of iniquity to overflowing.

CHAPTER TWENTY

———

"When my service here is o'er;

And this temporal tent, no more;

Give me the grace to walk the 'vale

And wings with which to fly to Thee;

That I might reach my heavenly home,

To kneel and worship at your throne"

CORNELIUS, BISHOP OF CAESAREA, ONCE an honourable soldier and centurion of Rome, returned to the city of his birth in the January of 68 AD. The dreadful news of the fire of Rome inspired in him a desire to help with the rebuilding programme and, although more than three years had passed since the sad event, there was still much work to be done. He arrived at the time of Nero's renewed attack against the church and so he also gave himself to helping the Christian population in their affliction. His Roman pedigree offered a modicum of security from the obvious danger he was in as a servant of Jesus Christ, as also did his military record, but he was, nevertheless, in considerable jeopardy as he made contact with church leaders and busied himself with ministering to the thousands of suffering saints. He soon became aware that his old friend Peter was also active in Rome and looked forward to arranging a reunion with the man who had led him to Jesus. Before this could materialise, however, he was arrested for his activities as a Christian and accused of being a traitor to Rome.

At the summit of the Fagutales, one of the Esquiline Hill's three peaks, stood the Praefectura Urbis (or Palace of Justice). Beneath the chambers were the dismal, foul smelling cells, for the housing of the remand prisoners before they were sent for trial. Many Christians were tried here, before being taken to the nearby Templum Telluris to be sentenced to death. Cornelius was no exception. His rights as a Roman were disregarded, considered forfeit because of what was considered to be treasonable conduct. He found himself chained in a cell with no natural light, keeping company with three other prisoners and innumerable vermin. He was now in his seventieth year and his bones ached in the damp conditions. He knew that he was living his last days on earth, but his spirit was alive and rejoicing in the presence and love of his Lord. Soon he would meet, face to face, the Saviour he had served so faithfully for almost thirty years and the anticipation of that awesome occasion, eclipsed the shadow of death which was now falling across his life.

The cries of a tortured church rose to the ears of the Almighty like the cries of Israeli slaves had done in Egypt long ago. The smell of burning flesh rose into the night sky from the gardens of Nero. His brand new "Golden House" now stood on the Palatine Hill surrounded by beautiful parkland and sporting flower gardens and vineyards. In front of his spectacular new house, he built a 30m high bronze statue of himself which became known as the Colossus. It overlooked an artificial lake which marked the centre of the garden. Here, in the place of natural beauty, Nero gloried in the shedding of blood and laid the foundation for the future persecution of the church. Ironically, it was upon this ground, eventually reclaimed from Nero's lake, that Emperor Vespasian would begin building the great amphitheatre (Coliseum) in 72 AD, in which so many Christians would be slaughtered, by being thrown to the lions.

Peter, now experiencing near exhaustion, redoubled his efforts. The commission given to him by his Lord, spurred him on. "Feed my lambs … feed my sheep" echoed and re-echoed in his mind. Joanna noticed that he was also writing another letter to the churches in Asia. She liked to read his letters. They had a special inspiration about them, which instructed and lifted her spirit. She found where he had written, "Shortly, I must put off this my tabernacle, even as our Lord Jesus Christ hath shown me. Moreover I will endeavour that you may be able after my decease to have these things always in remembrance." Joanna dropped the manuscript to the floor and held her hand to cover her mouth. Tears jerked into her eyes. He was saying that he was soon to die. That is why he was working so hard! He knew that his time on earth was short! He was extracting the last bit of service from his earthly tabernacle, before he laid it aside forever. How long did he have? Months? Perhaps a year? She dried her eyes and knelt humbly before her Lord.

"However long it is Lord, I will give my all. I will work hand in hand with Peter, until it is time for us to leave this earthly home and join you in everlasting bliss."

When the axe fell, it came in the most unexpected fashion, for it was not Peter who was first called to account, but his wife. The power behind the persecution, expert in psychological cruelty as well as physical, knew how to hurt

Peter the most. The Roman military burst unexpectedly into their humble home and seized Joanna. There was no opportunity for a kiss goodbye, no merciful moments of farewell, only the brutal tearing away of a wife from her husband. Joanna was a godly soul and, not for the first time in her life, she remained calm and resolute in the face of affliction. She even managed a reassuring smile at Peter as she was roughly escorted from the house. He is reported to have called after her, "My dear Joanna, remember the Lord" (viii) and she was gone from him and from the world. He never saw her again. The woman, who had so often been a willing host to Jesus back in her home at Capernaum, ministering to Him in the days of His ministry, was ushered into His eternal presence with unspeakable joy and Peter was left to mourn her loss. He wept for her until he was dry of tears. His heart searched for her in his dreams, wandering the dark alleyways of Rome, crying out her name, but never finding her. Once he did! She ran into his arms and he held her warmth close to him and sobbed onto her shoulder. But then he woke, weeping into his pillow, and experienced the pain of unutterable loss.

Paul was the next victim of Nero's attention. Peter visited him only once, in the prison within the Emperor's palace. It was quite a visit. The two ageing warriors of the Kingdom talked of Jesus and His work, rejoicing together in the thousands of converts to Christ who were now spreading the Gospel across the earth. They were so different in background and upbringing, yet closer than natural brothers. They had served the same Lord for many years, one a little longer than the other, and their fruit followed them. After a lengthy period of imprisonment, Paul was now called to trial for his life. As a Roman citizen he was entitled to a proper trial, before

Nero himself, and so was brought, in chains, to stand before the emperor.

It is regrettable that nobody was with Paul on the day of his trial, either to give him moral support or to take record of the proceedings for posterity, but we can be assured that he gave a good account of himself, the Gospel, and righteousness. He was a hunched little figure, older than his years and bearing the marks of much adversity, but he was as spiritually and mentally as alert as ever. What a contrast they presented, Nero, servant of Satan, and Paul, the servant of Jesus Christ. God and the personification of evil faced each other in two of their most dedicated servants. The pompous, debased youth, and the aged warrior of truth, one with all the power of the natural world, the other with the power of a world unseen. Light and darkness faced each other, purity contested heinous filth. Foolishness pitted itself against Holy Ghost wisdom, and dignity smiled at intemperance. When injustice finally prevailed and Paul was sentenced to death, his victory was sealed in his uncompromising response. Nero saw in the eyes of this old Jew, the smile of another world, the confidence of one who knew where he had been and where he was going, and was satisfied with both. It was a strange irony that the thirty year old young man who so flippantly committed Paul to die, would within a few weeks lose his own life in a panic suicide.

It was during the trial of Paul that Nero moved to arrest Peter. It was not unexpected and Peter was fully prepared. He knew that any trial that he might be given would be brief and that its conclusion would be a death sentence. He could have left Rome at any time over those last weeks, but he knew, for a number of reasons, that it was not right to do so. He believed that it was time for him to finally make amends for his great mistake in the judgement hall of Caiaphas. There would be no running from this, no denial of his Lord. He was ready to lay down his life for Jesus. He was taken to the Praefectura Urbis and committed to a dark damp underground cell in the basement. The jailor pushed him in the back with his foot as he entered and Peter fell headlong, grazing his head on the stone wall. It was cold and filthy and it took several minutes for his eyes to adjust to the half light. A fellow prisoner kindly helped him into a sitting position and dabbed the wound with his sleeve.

"Are you in pain?" he asked. "Here, take my coat to sit on, it will insulate you from the cold."

Peter smiled at the man's kindness.

"You must be a follower of Jesus," he said to the stranger. "That's the kind of thing He taught us to do."

"Indeed I am sir, and have been these last three decades, ever since the Lord graciously sent His servant to my home in Caesarea, back in Israel, to preach to me the Gospel, even though I was a Gentile sinner."

Peter stiffened. His mind flashed back to the magnificent home of a Roman centurion in Caesarea and to a vision of unclean animals descending from the heavens for him to eat. He took hold of the wrists of his fellow prisoner and searched the man's bearded face through the gloom.

"Is your name Cornelius?" he asked.

A few moments later and they were laughing and crying in each other's arms. It was an unlikely scene, two elderly men dancing with the joy of their reunion in a dark, cold prison cell. They sat and reminisced about their first God-ordained encounter and updated each other on their experiences as preachers of the Word of God, across the years. The Roman and the Jew, the bishop of Caesarea and the bishop of Rome, the centurion and the fisherman, they chattered like school boys until they fell asleep.

It was but a few days before their companionship was ended. The guards came to escort Cornelius to his place of execution. He still knew how to hold himself erect in true military style and his eyes betrayed no fear. Peter stood to embrace his convert of long ago, with the love of a true brother.

"Be brave, my friend," he whispered. "Soon you will be free of the pains of this world and enjoying the bliss of the Eternal Presence, absent from the body and present with the Lord." Cornelius, his arms heavy with chains, walked to the door, turned and looked back at the fisher of men. The flickering light from the guard's torch was rippling across the scarred face of the old soldier. He smiled.

"See you soon, Peter."

Nero took sadistic pleasure in arranging for both Paul and Peter to die on the same day. It was the 29th June 68 AD and Nero was giddy with childish anticipation as he rose from his bed. Today he would rid Rome and the world, of its two most prominent Christian leaders. He positioned himself in royal pomp and youthful arrogance and ordered that the prisoner be paraded past his vantage point on his way to execution. He grinned and pointed, as Paul, led by a centurion and flanked with soldiers, was marched past him, to leave the city of Rome for the final time. The prisoner looked neither to the right, nor to the left, but walked with the dignity of a monarch. He was somewhat hunched, worn by affliction, and limping, but his demeanour was that of the son of a King. It was an unremarkable scene as they walked a considerable distance along the road to Ostia. Hundreds of people thronged the route, all about their daily business and very few of them even sparing the time to glance at yet another prisoner being led to execution. But heaven watched as one of its favourite sons was given a military escort to his departure point, like Jesus before him, outside the city walls. Ranks of angels stood in awe as another loyal servant of Jesus Christ began his final journey home.

The centurion called the company to halt at a place called Tre Fontane, and there Paul knelt one final time on earth, in submission to his Lord. He committed his soul into the hands of the Saviour and fixed his attention on the world he had previewed twenty two years before in a near death experience at Lystra. He then lifted his voice and quoted the words he had recently written to his friend Timothy at Ephesus.

"I am now ready to be offered, and the time of my departure is at hand. I have fought a good fight, I have finished my course; I have kept the faith."

He bowed his head. The sword of the executioner flashed in the sunlight and freed the spirit of Paul to fly to his beloved. Suffering over, he found rest in the presence of Jesus.

For Peter, who had no claim to Roman citizenship, the passage to heaven was to be more painful, and more entertaining to his evil persecutor. Like his Lord before him, he was to be crucified. He had come a long way since that morning on the beach when Jesus made them all breakfast and challenged Peter three times, "Lovest thou me?" As they walked away from the lakeside that day Jesus had said to him, "Follow thou me", just as he had done when all this began, at Capernaum three years before. And he had! He had followed Him faithfully ever since and he followed Him to the end. Now the words that Jesus spoke to him as they walked across the shingle that day were about to come to pass. "When thou shalt be old, thou shalt stretch forth thy hands, and another shall gird thee, and carry thee whither thou wouldest not." This Jesus had spoken, "signifying by what death he should glorify God."

The place of execution was Nero's garden, in the Vallis Vaticana, the scene of the mass martyrdom of hundreds of the followers of the Lord Jesus. It was to be a public spectacle, watched from his imperial box by the emperor himself, together with his bloodthirsty cohorts. The command was given for Peter to be brought from his cell beneath the Palace of Justice and half an hour later he appeared in chains. He was roughly pushed into the centre of the arena and fell sprawling in the mud. In doing so he became entangled in his bonds and the crowd roared with laughter. Nero stood and clapped his hands gleefully, turning and making comments to the woman at his side. Peter was pulled to his feet and dragged towards a crudely erected wooden X frame. The clothes were then ripped from his body, until he stood naked before the people. Once more a roar of laughter filled the midday air. They then proceeded to strap his wrists and ankles to the frame with leather thongs. The crucifixion was to be preceded by the usual scourging of the victim.

Peter had already experienced the pain of a Jewish flogging, on the day that he and his friend John were brought before the Sanhedrin, but now the cruelty of Rome would be applied to open up those old scars. The instrument of torture was called a flagellum and consisted of a wooden handle to which were fastened three leather strips, often studded with small pieces of metal designed to tear the prisoners flesh. The executioner was a tall burly man with the strength of an ox and the eyes of a caged lion. He took the flagellum in one hand and, swinging his whole weight behind the blow, applied it to Peter's naked back. The mob howled its approval and Nero grinned triumphantly.

Peter was just sixty nine years old. His previously strong physical frame was now much weakened with the passing years and there was not so much flesh on his frame, as in his earlier years. The lash soon cut him to the bone and the blood flowed freely into the damp sod. Unconsciousness provided a sweet, but temporary release. Alarmed by the obvious loss of blood, Nero warned that they should take care not to kill him under the scourge. Such would cut short the entertainment. He wanted to watch this hated Christian die slowly. Long intervals elapsed between the lashes, but still they fell, as they had done upon the back of the Redeemer years before. So much of this reminded Peter of the path his Lord had taken; the roar of the crowd, the mocking, the nakedness, the Roman soldiers, the scourging, and now the cross and the heat of the noonday sun. This is what he had shunned and run away from thirty one years before. He was willing now! From the cross, he could not, would not, turn away. Only one thing troubled him! He felt so unworthy to die as his Lord had died! This was all too similar to the happenings on Golgotha and he felt that he had no right to walk such a path of holiness and sacrifice.

He was no Saviour, just a Saviour's servant. He counted it a privilege to share in the fellowship of His sufferings, but not to die as He, the Saviour of the world, had died.

They began to strap him to the cross upon which he was destined to die. Through bruised and bloodied lips he spoke to his persecutors.

"Permit me this one thing," he implored. "Allow me to be crucified head down!"

The soldiers looked at each other and grinned with disbelief. What kind of crazy man would make such a request? Was the pain, the shame, the horror, not enough already? What foolishness would drive a man to add yet more agony to his cup of affliction? One of them walked across to the centurion and after a few seconds muttered conversation, the latter made an approach to the emperor.

Nero laughed uproariously! No problem! Of course the Jewish fanatic could be inverted! What better way to add a little more amusement to the afternoon's entertainment, than for this absurd Christian to be yet more humiliated.

So they did! They hung this faithful servant of Jesus up to die, naked and alone. Alone, that is, except for the presence of Jesus, who seemed so close, that Peter felt that he could feel His very breath. When Jesus died, He was truly alone, for even His Father turned away, in order that, as by one man sin entered the world, one man should make atonement. But Peter was not alone. Jesus was with him, in him, moment by moment, sharing the burden of his cross. Heaven fell silent and the angels stood, amazed to watch the spectacle of the man, who once cursed and swore that he did not know Jesus, now so willingly embrace his cross.

The blood pounded in his head, eyes bulged and blurred with pressure, pain tortured every nerve and sinew of his body, and the sound of laughter filled his ears. He could hear Nero squealing with excitement as he gratified his lust for cruel pleasure in this crude and absurd sight. The heat of the summer sun brought no balm to his burning flesh and his tortured lungs found it more and more difficult to find the necessary air. Perspiration and blood conspired together and stung his burning eyes. He thought of the morning on the beach, when Jesus asked him if he loved Him. He had been so hesitant in his reply that day, so soon after he had failed. Now, through his agony, his lips formed the faintest of smiles, and through his broken and parched lips he whispered a present answer to the question from long ago.

"Yea Lord, thou knowest that I love thee."

The pain was easing a little now and the shouting of the crowd was not quite so loud. He was not sure at first, but he thought he could hear something else, like a distant sound of music. He tried to tune his ear, to discern its origin. It was the sound of far away singing, like the sound of huge choirs in the skies above. As he listened, it seemed that the music drew nearer. He blinked his eyes to see if he could see them, but there was too much blood. Then his hearing became suddenly acute and he could clearly hear the music! It was like music he had never heard before; the chords, the harmonies, the diversity of instruments, the sweet blend of majestic music, a great symphony of sound which appeared to fill the heavens with the Glory of God. What could this be? He could see now! It was as though he was flying low over rolling pastures and green meadows. There were soft rising hills of indescribable beauty, skies of transparent blue, and lakes, lakes which surpassed in beauty even his beloved Galilee. The colours, the flowers, the perfume of this paradise, brought tears to his eyes, and the pain was gone now, forgotten forever.

Then he saw them, Cherubim and Seraphim, millions of angelic beings, resplendent in their magnificence, clothed in glittering white and standing around the throne of God and of the Lamb. The light was awesome, an ethereal light, which, though brighter than anything he had ever seen before, was gentle to the eyes. The music was coming from around the throne, where, not only angels stood, but millions of others, who had been redeemed from the earth. His heart was dancing, intoxicated with joy. Laughter filled his soul. He looked down and saw that he was arrayed in the most wonderful white raiment. The material was as gentle as gossamer, reflecting the glory which poured like waves of light from the throne of God.

Peter moved, or rather was gently carried, by unseen hands, towards the assembled throng. He would have been quite content to join their number at the rear, to add his voice to the song, which, although it was one he had never heard before, he felt that he already knew. Such, however, was not to be. As he approached that innumerable company, it began to part, gently, like a receding wave, to form an avenue through the assembled throng, a wide isle of love, which pointed to the throne. Peter found himself walking slowly through the saints and angels, eyes forward, searching for the One he had longed for so long to see. And there He was, standing to greet His friend, Jesus of Nazareth, the man of

John Hibbert

Galilee, pulsating with the glory he deserved. He held out both his arms to His faithful servant.

"Welcome, Peter," Jesus said, "Enter thou into the joy of thy Lord."

ADDENDUM

(i) Dionysius wrote in 170 AD "Peter came to Italy, and, having taught there, suffered martyrdom".

Clement spoke of "What Peter had taught in Rome".

Irenaeus claimed that Peter and Paul "entrusted the bishopric of Rome to Linus".

Tertullian made reference to "those whom Peter baptised in the Tiber".

(ii) "Upon this Rock".

These words of the Lord Jesus are the subject of huge controversy between the Roman Catholic and Protestant wings of Christendom. The Roman Catholic theologians have developed the statement of Jesus to mean that here our Lord was establishing Peter as the first Pope and that all succeeding Popes are the successors of Peter. In opposition to papist doctrines the Protestant church has set itself to deny that Jesus was meaning Peter when He said "Upon this rock". With considerable manoeuvring of scripture to suit their ends, such Bible students claim that Jesus was not referring to Peter, but to the statement which Peter had just made about Jesus, that He was "The Christ, the Son of the living God". Others claim that He was directly referring to Himself, saying, "Thou art Peter" (Pointing to Peter) and "Upon this rock" (Pointing to Himself) "I will build my church". They make use of original Greek words (the language used in the writing of the New Testament) to support these theories, pointing out that two separate words were used, one translated "Peter" and the other translated "rock". Roman Catholics are happy to talk about the original words in Greek and Aramaic (the language that Jesus actually spoke).

"Thou art Peter" – The Greek word for Peter is "Petros"

"Upon this rock" – The word for "rock" is "Petra"

We need to understand here that Jesus is using the analogy of His church as a building, built upon foundations. The Greek word for "rock" is "Petra" so He says He will build His church on "this petra." If He wishes to call Simon, "the rock" upon which He builds, He cannot use the word "Petra", as it is a word with the feminine gender. It would not be fitting to call a man by a female name. So to complete His analogy Jesus uses the male counterpart of the word, "Petros". There is nothing more significant or sinister in the change of words than that. It was to do with gender. The controversy is finally resolved, however, by pointing out that, although the New Testament was written in Greek, Jesus actually conversed in Aramaic. In Aramaic there is no masculine and feminine gender for words and the word for "rock" is "Cephas". So what Jesus actually SAID to Peter was, "Thou art 'Cephas', and upon this 'Cephas' I will build my church. There can be no doubt that Jesus was addressing Peter, about Peter, and that He was putting upon this man a huge responsibility. This does not mean that Roman Catholics are correct to turn this verse into support for papist doctrines. They should remember that the church is "built upon the foundation of the apostles and prophets, Jesus Christ Himself being the chief corner stone" (Eph.2:20). Peter was addressed in Mtt.16:18, but his calling was not exclusive.

The Protestant church should recognise the danger of undermining truth through fear and, as a consequence, excuse itself from God given responsibility. Jesus will build His church, but only through people. Like Peter we are called to be foundations in our generation and the keys of the kingdom have been placed within our hands. If we take the responsibility, and the keys, away from Peter, we hide behind our own deception and fail to rise to the challenge ourselves. Jesus gave to Peter great authority in these verses, an authority which has passed, not to the pope, but to all those who claim to be the servants of Jesus Christ. We fail to use it at our peril.

(iii) The Bema

Bema is a Greek word meaning "step" and was the raised pulpit area which occupied the central position of the Jewish Synagogue. Its origins in Greek culture go back to Athens where the Bema was used as a speaking platform for orators, with particular reference to law and judgment. Its adoption into the Jewish Synagogue was fitting in that it was used for the reading and exposition of the sacred scriptures and the Law of Moses, which is the standard and pattern for the judgment of humankind. In Christianity it represents the eternal judgment of the church by the Lord Jesus. Paul says, "We must all appear before the judgment seat (Greek, "Bema") of Christ; that every one may receive the things done in his body, according to that he hath done, whether it be good or bad." (2Cor.5:10). It is significant that Jesus read the portion from Isaiah which related to mercy, compassion and healing, but stopped short of completing the sentence "… and the day of vengeance of our God." He was reading as the Saviour of the World, but from the symbol of judgment. It was not time for Him to announce judgment, but its future application was implied by the pulpit upon which He stood. He is the only One qualified to judge in eternity, because He already paid, as the Saviour, for the forgiveness of all who trust and obey Him.

(iv) Jesus presented Himself as the supreme master of everything, the One to whom nothing is impossible, but He did not force Himself upon His servants. He was available for any one of those men to join Him on the water, but He did not push them, or even suggest it. He began to walk away! It was Peter's desire to walk with Jesus in the miraculous, followed up by a bold commitment to do it, which brought the invitation from the Lord. So many Christians and churches cling fastidiously to their battered boats, waiting for Jesus to climb on board and work miracles inside the ship. He will not! He is seeking to entice His people to venture into the impossible, outside our comfort zone. When we are serious about getting out of the boat, He will give us the word of faith upon which to stand.

(v) Satanic opposition to the church and to individual servants of Jesus Christ is complex and sinister. It should never be treated flippantly. It should be noted that the Lord Jesus treated this matter with agonising seriousness. The people of God do not wrestle against flesh and blood, but against an organised structure of evil power which is terrifyingly real. Christians and ministers who insolently and ignorantly yell their commands at satanic power are committing an act of huge folly. It is significant that Jesus promised to pray for Peter, that his faith would not fail in the conflict. If the Master of the Universe needed to pray, do we think that by arranging a church march around a city we can unseat powers that may have been established for generations? It is only by prolonged prayer and fasting that the demonic world is overcome. We are assured of victory, but only if we are prepared to pay the price!

(vi) It is a tragedy of enormous proportions that the church has historically fought over inconsequential details, whilst its commission to preach the Gospel to the world has been so seriously neglected. Fragmented into denominations and groups, fighting over minor points of doctrine and even squabbling over territory, the church has repeatedly sunk its fishing boats with tradition and schisms, until its power to affect the world becomes non existent. The last moments of opportunity for the church to win the lost will only be successful if Christians put aside their differences, cease to major on incidentals, and in the unity of the Spirit of Christ present the message of salvation in the power of the Holy Ghost.

(vii) The Nicene Creed of 325 AD was compiled in the face of a heresy promoted by a Libyan preacher by the name of Arius. He claimed that the Son of God was created by God, not begotten of God from one substance, thus contradicting the doctrine of the Trinity. The creed consisted of the following statement of faith:-

"We believe in one God, the Father Almighty, Maker of all things visible and invisible. And in one Lord Jesus Christ, the Son of God, begotten of the Father (the only begotten;

that is, of the essence of the Father, God of God, Light of Light, very God of very God) begotten not made, being of one substance with the Father; by whom all things were made (both in heaven and on earth); who for us men, and for our salvation, came down and was incarnate and was made man; He suffered, and on the third day he rose again, ascended into heaven; From thence he shall come to judge the quick and the dead. And in the Holy Ghost."

(viii) The story of the martyrdom of Peter and his wife is found in the pages of The History of the Church, written by Eusebius, a bishop in the Holy Land during the first decades of the 300s.

In it he quotes from a much earlier source, Miscellanies (Book VII), written by Clement of Alexandria (circa A.D. 150–215). This work describes how Peter's wife suffered martyrdom just before him: We are told that when blessed Peter saw his wife led away to death, he was glad that her call had come and that she was returning home, and spoke to her in the most encouraging and comforting way, addressing her by name: "My dear, remember the Lord."

Lightning Source UK Ltd.
Milton Keynes UK
26 November 2010

163515UK00001B/6/P